MW00667019

ED SAINDON

The

Complete Guide

To Improvisation

VOLUME 1

The Complete Guide To Improvisation

Ed Saindon

The Complete Guide to Improvisation codifies and explains the principal concepts and techniques as used by leading improvisors past and present.

- The guide is presented in a series of four volumes with 21 chapters in total. All the material is set out in a clear, concise and concentrated format which is easy to understand, absorb and assimilate.

- Written explanation of concepts, techniques and practice suggestions are balanced alongside relevant examples, practical routines and written solos.

- The material in this series offers practical improvisational techniques and concepts which will help musicians of all levels to expand and refine their skills in the art of improvisation.

For more information on *The Complete Guide to Improvisation*, please go to www.edsaindon.com

Working with The Complete Guide to Improvisation

1) For the many techniques in the series which focus on the upper extensions of the harmony (e.g. Four Note Groupings, Upper Structure Triads and Pentatonics) it is recommended to play the examples and written solos on the piano along with the harmony of the composition. Playing along with an accompaniment track is also effective.

2) Although the focus of the series is on improvisation concepts, all players must also be constantly aware of their sound in terms of articulation, nuance, dynamics and sense of phrasing when playing the lines. Playing along with a metronome on 2 and 4 is also recommended.

3) Most of the lines in the book use eighth note rhythms for ease of reading and a clear focus on improv concepts. However, once the improv technique is assimilated the player should utilize a greater variety of rhythms along with the use of syncopation and space (for more information on rhythm, please refer to my books *Rhythmic Phrasing* and *Advanced Rhythms in Improvisation,* both published by Advance Music).

4) Transposing examples to other keys, scales and chords is beneficial. The assimilation of an improv concept or technique in playing is also greatly helped by writing out solos utilizing that specific concept or technique. I would then recommend improvising with a single technique or combination of techniques over a particular chord progression or composition.

Series Background

I have been fortunate to be on the Faculty at Berklee College of Music in Boston since 1976, teaching in the areas of improvisation, ensembles and private instruction. The many years of teaching and performing have given me valuable experience and enabled me to judiciously select and codify the improvisational concepts and techniques in this guide.

The initial motivation to write this series of books on improvisation was primarily as a means of personal growth as an improvisor. Through recordings, discussions with players, and transcription analysis, this is the outcome. The project has now been going on for well over five years, and I have thoroughly enjoyed the process. Most importantly, I feel it has had a major impact on my playing.

Biography

Ed Saindon entered Berklee College of Music in 1972 as a drummer, studying with Alan Dawson and Gary Chaffee. During his sophomore year, he began studying with Gary Burton on vibraphone and piano. Ed graduated Magna Cum Laude in 1976, at which time he joined the faculty at Berklee at the invitation from Gary Burton. Ed's teaching activities as professor at Berklee include private lessons, ensemble performance and improvisation.

Ed Saindon is active as both a performer and composer. His last two recordings as a leader, *Key Play* with Kenny Werner and *Depth of Emotion* with Dave Liebman, have featured his own compositions.

Ed has also played and/or recorded with such players as Ken Peplowski, Warren Vache, Kenny Werner, Dave Liebman, Mick Goodrick, Fred Hersch, Peter Erskine, Jeff Hamilton, Louie Bellson, Herb Pomeroy, Dick Johnson, Howard Alden, Dave McKenna, Marvin Stamm, Michael Moore, Ed Thigpen, Adam Macowicz, George Masso, Dan Barrett, among others.

Ed remains open to all kinds of music and enjoys all styles from straight ahead standards to contemporary originals.

As a concert artist and clinician, Ed Saindon has travelled throughout the U.S., Europe, Brazil, Mexico and Japan.

In addition to teaching at Berklee College of Music and performing, Ed has produced numerous books, including *Berklee Practice Method: Vibraphone* published by Berklee Press, *Rhythmic Phrasing in Improvisation* and *Advanced Rhythms in Improvisation,* both published by Advance Music. Ed Saindon has also published many articles on music education, jazz theory and improvisation. His articles have appeared in many publications including Down Beat, Percussive Notes (Percussive Arts Society magazine) and Percussioner International. He is currently the vibraphone and jazz mallet editor for the Percussive Arts Society.

Acknowledgements

I was very fortunate to study with legendary drummer/educator Alan Dawson on entering Berklee College of Music. During my sophomore year, I saw Gary Burton perform at a commencement concert. Shortly after, I had Gary for a beginning mallet lab and later for private lessons. Upon graduating in 1976, I began teaching at the college at the age of 21. I was privileged to have Gary as a teacher/mentor and have the utmost gratitude for his support and inspiration through the years.

Joe Locke is an incredible vibist, deep musician and close friend. We have had many playing sessions and conversations on the subject of improvisation. Joe has always been very open about sharing his concepts and the material he is working on. These sessions and talks, as well as his inspirational playing, have been valuable and influential in building this project.

A very special thanks goes to another close friend, Gustavo Agatiello. Gustavo teaches with me at Berklee. He is a deep and musical vibist/musician. I respect his opinion and value his input. Gustavo has been an important part of this book from the very beginning. We have discussed techniques and concepts that have gone into this book. He is the sole person who has been in charge of putting the book together and getting it ready for production.

I had the opportunity to play with the late trumpeter Herb Pomeroy for many years in Boston. We had a long-standing Sunday brunch duo engagement at some of the hotels and restaurants in town. On those many gigs, Herb and I would play and talk about music. All those years playing with Herb were very influential in terms of my overall musical development. Herb was a great musician, educator and person. He is still sadly missed.

Lastly, other indirect influences on the book have been people that I have played with through the years. Hopefully as musicians, we never stop learning and growing. We can pick up big and little things playing with other musicians in the studio or on the bandstand. I have tried to learn from all of them.

Table of Contents

© 2012 by Ed Saindon Music
No parts of this publication may be reproduced, stored in a retrival system, or transmitted, in any form or by any means, electronically, mechanically, photocopying, recording, or otherwise, without prior written permission by Ed Saindon Music.

International copyright secured

Music typesetting: Ed Saindon & Gustavo Agatiello
Layout: Ed Saindon & Gustavo Agatiello
Cover art by Allison Sharpe

Production: Ed Saindon & Gustavo Agatiello

ISBN 978-0-9883974-0-8

Chord Tone Soloing

This is an important and fundamental approach to improvisation. The technique involves using only chord tones as a means of note selection. The challenge lies in the fact that chord tones are stable notes and consequently negate the ability to play with any degree of tension resolution. Therefore, in order to generate interest, variety and flow in the improvised line, it is vital that the improvisor resorts to the musical elements presented in this chapter.

Motives

Try to utilize and develop motives in the solo. Any phrase, whether it be two notes or ten notes can be a motive. Motives create a sense of interest in the solo and draw the listener in. It can be helpful to let the lines "breathe" and "pick up" motives along the way, as they appear and evolve throughout the solo. It also helps to avoid sounding every chord tone of the chord. Below is an example of chord tone soloing based upon a two bar progression in C Min. Notice how the chords are connected.

Regarding the use of motives in the solo: motives can be as simple as two notes.
The solo begins with a two-note minor 3rd interval. Notice how the motive is repeated in measure 3.
The three-note motive in the second half of the first measure is also repeated in the second half of the second measure (the motive is inverted). Also notice the repetitive motive (sequence) in measures 7 & 8. (Ex. 1)

For more on the use of motives, please refer to the chapter Motivic Playing.

Editing, Use of Space & Syncopation

Referring to letting the lines "breathe", the use of editing can be a valuable technique.
Editing involves being more selective in terms of note choices and deleting unnecessary and repetitive notes in a melodic line. The use of editing can make a melodic phrase more concise and coherent, allowing for more space and enabling the improvisor to apply more syncopated rhythms.
As a result, edited lines tend to have more impact on the listener. Here is an example that uses chord tones with no space. (Ex. 2A)

The following is an example illustrating the application of editing. Notice how the line in the above example becomes more interesting and displays a clearer sense of phrasing as a result of rhythm syncopation and use of space. (Ex. 2B)

Phrasing

Here are some suggestions with regard to phrasing: try to make the phrases connect from chord to chord and measure to measure without them sounding like separate ideas. Strive to phrase over the bar line, beginning and ending a phrase in unpredictable places in the measure as well as in the form of the composition. Vary the phrase lengths. Perhaps play a short phrase, leave space and play a longer phrase. Play a phrase over three bars instead of two bars (many improvisors will play in two bar phrases and maintain a predictable pattern of activity and rest). Experiment with varying the phrasing in this regard. For example, play a three bar phrase, and then play a two bar phrase starting in measure 4 of the composition. Try playing a two bar phrase starting in the 8th measure (many improvisors will play a two bar phrase in measures 7 & 8 and begin a new phrase in measure 9).

The following example contains over the bar line phrases that flow from one measure to the next. As previously discussed, notice the three bar phrase at the beginning of the solo. The next phrase is a two bar phrase that occurs in measures 4 and 5. Lastly, notice the two bar phrase in measures 8 and 9. (Ex. 3)

With the implementation of the aforementioned musical elements, chord tone soloing can be a very effective technique in improvisation. The goal should be to make the improvisation sound musical, as opposed to an academic exercise.

Additional Suggestions

• 	Avoid consistently starting with the root of the chord. Any chord tone can be used to begin a phrase.

• 	Avoid playing up and down arpeggios. This will make the improv seem like an exercise. Try to create lines with unusual and unexpected leaps and changes in direction. It's not necessary to play every chord tone of each chord.

• 	In terms of rhythm, strive for a balance of non-syncopated and syncopated figures, as well as using a variety of rhythms that may include 8th notes, triplets and 16th notes. Also, try to balance the line with the use of long notes and short notes.

Suggested Exercises

Here are some exercises to further help the improvisor incorporate the technique of chord tone soloing:

Chord Tone Connection

This method involves starting with the lowest note on your instrument and going up and down the instrument using only chord tones. When transitioning from one measure to the next, play the closest note in the new chord. You can begin by using quarter notes and then proceed to 8th notes, triplets and 16th notes. This example (using a 3 octave range beginning from F below middle C) is based upon the 1st 8 bars of a well-known standard. (Ex. 4A)

Playing Within an Octave

This technique entails staying within an octave while only using chord tones and consequently requires that the improvisor see the chords in various inversions. (Ex. 4B)

Second's Notice Chord Tone Solo

The following solo is based on a John Coltrane standard and illustrates the sole use of chord tones along with musical elements that have been previously discussed. Notice the manipulation of motives within the solo. The use of space and syncopation helps to avoid making the solo sound stiff and academic. Also notice how the phrases not only overlap the measures, but they also overlap the key changes. (Ex. 5)

Guide Tone Lines

A guide tone line is a stepwise line (usually moving by 1/2 steps) that leads smoothly through a progression and helps identify the quality of the chords. The line most often involves the 3rd and 7th of the chord (also called the guide tones), as these notes sound the quality of the chord.

Guide tone lines connect the chords of a progression via voice leading, and allow the improvisor to sound the changes with a minimum of chord tones. Classical composers such as J.S. Bach were masters with this technique.

The following example shows a very simple guide tone line that sounds the 3rd of each diatonic triad. This guide tone line, along with the root of the chord, will sound the chord progression. (Ex. 6A)

The next example displays a simple guide tone line that sounds the 7th of the Dom 7 going to the 3rd of the IV Maj chord of the key. The 3rd of the IV chord then goes down a 1/2 step to the 3rd of the IV Min chord. (Ex. 6B)

Multiple Guide Tone Lines

There is usually more than one guide tone line inherent in a chord progression. Here is the same progression as in the previous example along with an additional guide tone line. (Ex. 6C)

Most often, the guide tone line will proceed from measure to measure in descending 1/2 steps. In the following example, the guide tone line sounds the 3rds and 7ths while going down in 1/2 steps from measure to measure. (Ex. 6D)

In many progressions, it becomes necessary to shift to another guide tone in order to bring out a specific chord tone or a more effective line that sounds the changes. In the next example, the guide tone line alternates between the 3rd and 7th of each chord. This is necessary since the 3rd of F-7 is a common tone on the successive Bb-7 chord and consequently will not sound the change. (Ex. 6E)

A good exercise would be to play through all keys with all chord types and sound the 3rd and 7th of each chord. Here is an example of Dom 7th chords played through the cycle. (Ex. 6F)

Not all guide tone lines will necessarily always include the 3rd and/or 7th of the chord. In the following example the line begins with the 5th, proceeds up in 1/2 steps and then down in 1/2 steps. (Ex. 6G)

The strongest guide tone line in a II-7 V7 progression consist of the 7th of the II-7 chord going down a 1/2 step to the 3rd of the V7 chord. On the V7 to I chord, the 3rd of the V7 (the leading tone of the key) can resolve up a 1/2 step to the root of the I chord. The 7th of the V7 chord can also resolve down a 1/2 step to the 3rd of the I chord. (Ex. 6H)

Guide Tone Lines on Second's Notice

Here is an example of guide tone lines (comprised of the 3rd and 7th of the chords) based on the progression of the same Coltrane composition as in Ex. 5. (Ex. 6I)

As previously mentioned, not all guide tone lines will always sound the 3rd and 7th of the chord. Here are additional guide tone lines on the same composition. Notice how the guide tones are all connected by 1/2 steps at the many key changes in the composition. (Ex. 6J)

Guide Tone Line Solo on Second's Notice

Here is a solo based upon the guide tone line sketch in Ex. 6I. The solo utilizes the guide tone lines along with other chord tones. This is good practice for the improvisor. First, sketch out guide tone lines for a progression of a standard composition and then write out a solo based upon those guide tone lines. Suggestion: go back to the chord tone solo in Ex. 5 and review for guide tone motion throughout the solo. (Ex. 6K)

Solo Utilizing Designated Intervals on Second's Notice

Another aspect of chord tone soloing can involve working with specific intervals. This is conducive to strong motives that flow through the chord progression and clearly sound the changes. The following is a solo based upon the same Coltrane composition. The lines are limited to 1/2 or whole steps, and perfect 4th and perfect 5th intervals drawn from available chord tones. The exclusive use of these specific intervals creates a characteristic sound throughout the overall solo. (Ex. 7)

How Deep is the Sea Chord Tone Solo

The next example is a chord tone solo based on a well-known standard. Try to analyze and isolate the musical elements that have been discussed in this chapter. Specifically, look for guide tone motion, use of motives, phrase connection from measure to measure and use of space along with rhythmic syncopation. (Ex. 8)

Chord Tone Soloing is a fundamental technique of improvisation and a good way to begin improvising. Limiting the parameters to strictly chord tones allows the improvisor to concentrate on such fundamental issues as the use of guide tone lines, motives, phrasing and rhythmic variety. Once a good grasp of soloing with chord tones has been established, the improvisor can in due course begin to utilize passing/approach notes and tensions along with chord tones. For more on this topic, please refer to the chapter Tension Resolution.

Tension Resolution

Improvisational techniques can generally be divided into two categories: vertical and horizontal. Horizontal playing techniques such as Pentatonics, Four Note Groupings and Upper Structure Triads/7ths may or may not sound the harmony. Vertical improvisational techniques such as Tension Resolution (hereafter labeled TR), carefully address and sound the underlying harmony. Furthermore, TR techniques can also create strong melodic lines with a clear sense of forward momentum. The aforementioned horizontal techniques may also be more effective if used in conjunction with TR techniques.

In the application of TR, emphasis is placed on the resolution of non-chord tones (unstable notes that create tension) to chord tones (stable notes that resolve the tension). The tension is sounded by a non-chord tone and the release occurs when a non-chord tone is resolved to an adjacent chord tone (also referred to as a target note).

TR allows the improvisor to utilize any twelve notes over a chord. However, careful consideration should be given to every note, as unresolved notes may interfere with and possibly destroy the sound of the underlying chord. Very dissonant non-chord tones may sound wrong and outside of the changes if they are not properly resolved.

TR prevents stagnation in the melodic line, as the constant back and forth of tension and release keeps the line moving. Even when improvising on one chord, such as in a modal tune, the integration of TR provides a sense of forward momentum to the melodic line.

The Tension Resolution Principle

Chord tones are stable notes that outline and sound the harmony. Any notes other than chord tones produce tension that can subsequently be resolved up or down to an adjacent chord tone. Along with chord tones, any non-chord tone may be sounded and then resolved to an adjacent chord tone at some point in the measure. Non-chord tones fall in the categories of **Passing, Approach** notes and/or **Tensions.**

Once a non-chord tone is sounded, it need not be resolved immediately. Delaying the resolution prolongs the tension, thereby creating a sense of unpredictability and suspense in the melodic line. Such tension can also be resolved into the following chord.

We will address the various TR techniques in the following order:

- **Diatonic and Chromatic Passing Notes**

- **Diatonic Approach Notes**

- **Chromatic Approach Notes**

- **Combining Diatonic and Chromatic Approach Notes**

- **Combining Passing and Approach Notes**

- **Tensions**

Diatonic and Chromatic Passing Notes

This technique involves the use of diatonic and/or chromatic passing notes placed between two chord tones. Depending upon the choice of passing notes and where chord tones and passing notes fall in relation to the beat, the improviser can create lines that sound "in" or "out". Yet, since the passing notes do resolve to adjacent chord tones, the melodic line will consistently sound the underlying chord changes.

It is important to create motivic ideas in combination with this technique in order to generate interesting and engaging lines. Classical compositions relied heavily on the practice of outlining the chord progression along with passing notes. J.S. Bach was a master at it. The effectiveness of this technique is a result of the tension resolution principle. The passing note produces the tension and the resolution occurs when an adjacent stable chord tone is sounded.

Passing Note Options for Chords

Maj 6th

Diatonic and chromatic passing notes between chord tones for a C Maj 6th chord. (Ex. 1A)

The following scale, also called a Bebop scale, places the chord tones on the downbeats and the passing notes on the upbeats. (Ex. 1B)

Here is another example of a scale with more unconventional passing notes. Notice how the passing notes are different going up the scale and coming down. (Ex. 1C)

Maj 7th
Diatonic and chromatic passing notes between chord tones for a C Maj 7th chord. (Ex. 1D)

This example shows how conventional diatonic passing notes can yield an Ionian and Lydian scale. (Ex. 1E)

The following example shows how more unusual scales can be generated via the use of more chromatic and unconventional passing notes. (Ex. 1F)

Min 7th
Diatonic and chromatic passing notes between chord tones for a C Min 7th chord. (Ex. 1G)

Here is a conventional scale using diatonic passing notes. (Ex. 1H)

The following example illustrates the use of additional chromatic passing notes sounded on the downbeats thus emphasizing more tension over the underlying chord. (Ex. 1I)

Min 7th b5

Diatonic and chromatic passing notes between chord tones for a C Min 7th b5 chord. (Ex. 1J)

The following is a conventional scale using typical passing notes for a Min 7th b5 chord. (Ex. 1K)

Here is another example using more interesting passing notes placed on the downbeats.
(Ex. 1L)

Dom 7th
Diatonic and chromatic passing notes between chord tones for a C Dom 7th chord. (Ex. 1M)

The scale going up is called Bebop scale. Natural passing notes are used going up and altered passing notes going down. (Ex. 1N)

Ex. 1N

Here is an example that uses passing notes derived from the Altered scale. (Ex. 1O)

Ex. 1O

This is another example that utilizes both natural and altered passing notes along with delayed resolution of the passing notes. (Ex. 1P)

Ex. 1P

Dom 7th sus

Diatonic and chromatic passing notes between chord tones for a C Dom 7th sus chord. (Ex. 1Q)

Here is a scale for a Dom 7th sus that sounds more conventional passing notes. (Ex. 1R)

This next example sounds altered notes on the Dom 7th sus chord. (Ex. 1S)

Maj 7th #5
Diatonic and chromatic passing notes between chord tones for a C Maj 7th #5 chord. (Ex. 1T)

Here is an example that sounds conventional passing notes (from Lydian Augmented scale) on a
Maj 7th #5 chord. (Ex. 1U)

This is an example that sounds more unconventional passing notes.
Notice how the passing notes are different in the scale going up versus down. (Ex. 1V)

Sample Lines

The following are some scalar examples that illustrate the use of passing notes used to generate lines over chords and typical progressions. Try to analyze the selection of passing notes, their placement in relation to the beat and the points of resolution. (Ex. 1W)

Diatonic Approach Notes

Diatonic approach notes are notes in the underlying chord's corresponding scale that are adjacent above and below any chord tone. As with passing notes, diatonic approach notes can help create strong melodic lines that sound the chord, while at the same time provide a strong degree of forward momentum via the back and forth tension release.

Diatonic approach notes can sound varying degrees of tension. If the diatonic approach note is an available tension, it can be sounded longer and more prominently, thus placing more emphasis on the tension's color over the underlying chord. "Avoid" notes should be handled carefully. Here is a list of diatonic approach notes for C Maj 7th along with each approach note's function over the chord. (Ex. 2A)

Diatonic approach notes for a given type of chord are dependent upon which scale is used for the chord. For example, diatonic approach notes for a Maj 7th chord will be different for an Ionian scale versus a Lydian scale. (Ex. 2B)

Due to the resolution tendencies of specific notes in a chord scale, some diatonic approach notes are not good choices when incorporated in a line. For example, scale degree 4 on a Maj 7th chord tends to resolve down a 1/2 step to the 3rd of the chord. For that reason, in an Ionian scale, a diatonic approach from below to the 5th of the chord would not be an effective choice. However, in a Lydian scale, the #4 diatonic approach from below to the 5th of the chord would be a good choice. (Ex. 2C)

Here are examples of diatonic approach notes for various chord types (listed with the specific scale selection) in the key of C along with sample melodic lines utilizing the approach notes. (Ex. 2D)

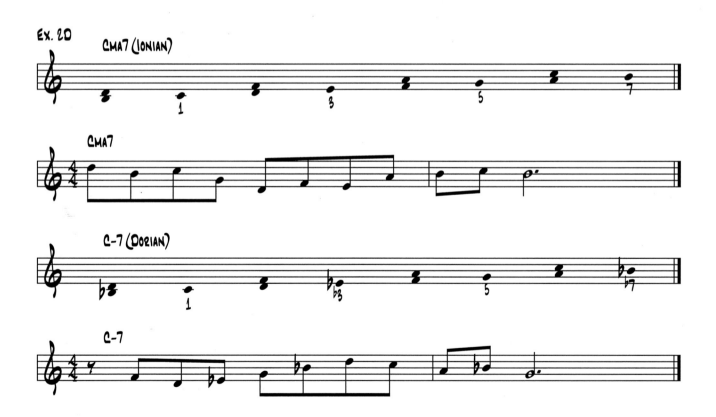

The following are sample lines utilizing diatonic approach notes on typical progressions. (Ex. 2E)

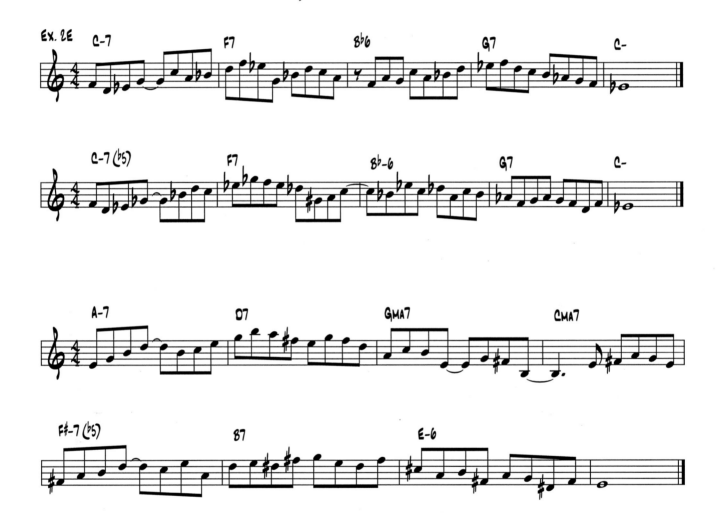

Diatonic Improvisation/Composition

Diatonic approach notes, along with diatonic passing notes, can be effective in creating clear and simple melodies for both improvisation and composition. The following short composition based on a simple harmonic progression features a melody constructed with diatonic approach and passing notes. The melody is created exclusively with an E Harmonic Minor scale. Notice how the melodic line clearly sounds the harmony, while the constant tension resolution creates a sense of forward momentum. It would be good practice to improvise in this manner on this or a similar progression using diatonic approach and passing notes. (Ex. 2F)

Improvisation with diatonic passing and approach notes can also be effective on pop style progressions. This is an example of diatonic lines over a typical pop style progression in the key of D Major. (Ex. 2G)

Chromatic Approach Notes

The following section will address the use of chromatic approach notes as a means of generating tension resolution. This is a fundamental improvisational technique that has been used in all styles of jazz, from the Swing and Bebop era up through the present. It is also worth noting that this technique has been used extensively in classical music. The interesting thing about the application of chromatic approach is that depending upon how the technique is applied, the improvisation can sound very stylistic and derivative if so desired, or more fresh and contemporary. The principle is that any chord tone can be approached from a 1/2 step below or above.

The chromatic approach note can be an integral component of the line and have a great deal of impact, since the melodic line's tension is created by the chromatic approach note(s).

Some specific details about chromatic approach: the improvised line may sound more consonant ("in") or more dissonant ("out") depending upon the choice of a specific chromatic note, whether or not the approach note is emphasized and/or held, and whether or not the chromatic approach note is sounded on the downbeat vs. the upbeat. Chromatic approach notes from below are generally more common than those from above, although 1/2 step approach notes from above on a Dominant chord are very effective. Note: a 1/2 step approach note from above to the root and 5th on a Dominant chord are tensions b9 and b13 respectively.

Here are two basic examples that illustrate the use of chromatic approach notes. Notice how the tension is created via the 1/2 step approach notes and subsequently released as the adjacent chord tones are sounded. (Ex. 3A)

The next example illustrates the use of chromatic approach succeeded by direct resolution immediately after the approach note is played. (Ex. 3B)

Here is the use of a chromatic approach note to the 3rd of each Dom 7th chord. (Ex. 3C)

Placing the approach notes on the downbeats accentuates the tension, which results in more dissonance in the line. (Ex. 3D)

Double Chromatic Approach Notes

A chord tone can also be approached via double chromatic approach from above and/or below. The following example illustrates the use of double chromatic approach to every chord tone on a D Min 7th chord. (Ex. 3E)

Various Double Chromatic Approach Patterns

The improvisor has many options to create patterns when using the four notes associated with double chromatic approach. Here are some examples of possible approaches to the 3rd of a D Min 7th chord. (Ex. 3F)

Combining Diatonic and Chromatic Approach

The combination of diatonic and chromatic notes enables the improvisor to expand the number of approach notes over a chord and consequently to create a great variety of approach patterns.

The following example on an F6 chord illustrates the use of diatonic and chromatic approach notes to the target note (in this case, the 3rd of the chord). Notice how the Bb functions as both a diatonic and a chromatic approach note. (Ex. 4A)

This next example shows the combination of both types of approach notes. A general rule in creating these patterns is that the diatonic approach notes should precede the chromatic approach notes. (Ex. 4B)

Here is an example that illustrates the use of both diatonic and chromatic approach notes to the 6th of the F6 chord. (Ex. 4C)

Here is another example combining both types of approach notes to the 6th of the F6 chord. Notice how the first 3 beats in the measure sound the approach notes with the consequent resolution occurring on the 4th beat. (Ex. 4D)

The following are sample lines that show the use of diatonic and chromatic approach notes over common progressions. (Ex. 4E)

More Approach Techniques

Approach Note Pattern Anticipation

The target note's approach notes can be sounded in the measure previous to that of the target note.
(Ex. 5A)

Approaching Scale Notes and/or Tensions

Not only can approach notes target chord tones, but also scale notes and/or tensions in the line. In this manner, more chromaticism can be obtained, allowing the improvisor to potentially sound all twelve notes over any chord. As illustrated in the following examples, target notes may include the 4th scale degree, tensions #11 and b13 on a Dom 7th chord, as well as tensions 9 and 11 on a Min 7th. (Ex. 5B)

Extreme Delayed Resolution

Approach notes to multiple target notes can be delayed and resolved later in the measure. This creates a sense of heightened dissonance that is released by sounding all the necessary target notes at the end of the measure. (Ex. 5C)

Combining Approach Notes/Passing Notes

By combining approach and passing notes, the improvisor can create highly chromatic and weaving lines over a chord. In the following examples illustrating this technique, determine the target notes and analyze where the passing notes, approach notes and the corresponding resolution points occur. (Ex. 5D)

Approach Note/Passing Note Patterns

The combination of approach and passing note patterns allows the improvisor the ability to create more expansive patterns. An effective technique is to target every chord tone in the chord with the use of approach notes and passing notes. In this next example, the chord tones of an Eb-6 chord are targeted. Keep in mind that these approach patterns to the target notes of Eb-6 could also be applied over other chords, as shown below. (Ex. 5E)

F7 sus | F7
C-7 b5 | F7
C7 | C7
G-7 b5 | C7

Similarly, we can target every chord tone of a chord in a progression. In the following example, the chord tones are sounded in a downward manner, which creates a gradual fall in the line.
This example could also be applied over the progressions shown below. (Ex. 5F)

D7 | G7 | C-
Eb7 sus | Ab7 | Db6
G7 sus | C7 sus | F-6

As previously mentioned in Ex. 5B, the improvisor can also use other scale degrees or tensions as target notes. In the following example, the notes of a D Dom 7th b9 are used as target notes. This line could be applied to many other chords, including: F7, Ab7, B7, C7, Gb7, Eb°7, Gb°7, A°7 and C°7 (Ex. 5G)

The improvisor can minimize the amount of target notes per chord by placing more emphasis on a greater number of passing and approach notes. In the following example, the majority of the notes in each measure consist of passing or approach notes. The target note is sounded in the very end of the measure. Although the line was intended for B-7 E7 A-, it could also be applied to other II-7 V7s, as illustrated below. (Ex. 5H)

C-7 b5 | F7 | Bb-6
A-7 | D7 | G-6

This next example displays a gradually rising line created via the ascending placement of the target notes. Other possible chord progressions for this line are shown below. (Ex. 5I)

D-7 | Db7 | C-6
C-7 b5 | F7 | Bb-6

Passing and approach notes can add substantial chromaticism to an improvised melodic idea. In the examples below, notice how those highly chromatic lines weave in and out of the tonality. However, all of the passing and approach notes are resolved. (Ex. 5J)

(For more information on this topic, please refer to the Approach Concepts & Techniques chapter).

Tensions

The improvisational idea can be based on the use of tension notes and their resolution to the underlying harmony. Utilizing tension notes as a basis to initiate lines is an important technique with inherent flux and potential to create harmonically rich melodies. With this TR concept, the focus is on the emphasis of a conventional or unconventional tension note, its placement in the measure, the specific beat it occurs on and how long it is sustained.

Tension Resolution Tendencies

The improvisor should be cognizant with the resolution tendencies of particular tensions. Most tensions can resolve up or down to the neighboring chord tone. However, some tensions have a specific resolution tendency. Here is a chart of those specific tension resolution tendencies:

#11 resolves up to the 5th
b9 resolves down to the root
#9 resolves up to the 3rd
b13 resolves down to the 5th

The following is a simple example of tension resolution on a II-7 V7. Tension 11 (G) on the D-7 resolves to the 3rd (F) and tension 13 (E) on the G Dom 7 resolves to the 5th (D). (Ex. 6A)

Delayed Resolution

A tension need not be immediately resolved. It can be resolved at any point during the measure or even into the next measure on the following chord. (Ex. 6B)

Multiple Tensions in a Measure

Multiple tensions can be sounded during the same measure on a chord. In the following example, the G7 sounds tensions 13 (E) and 9 (A). (Ex. 6C)

Natural and Altered Tensions in a Measure

Mixed use of natural and altered tensions is also possible, as illustrated in the following example. (Ex. 6D)

Lines Emphasizing Tensions

Beginning the measure with a tension immediately places the focus on the color of the chord and sets the line in forward motion. Here is an example based upon the first half of a well-known standard. The scalar lines begin by sounding an available tension in most of the measures. (Ex. 6E)

Unconventional Tensions

Sounding unconventional tensions can create a higher level of dissonance that can eventually be resolved to either a chord tone or a conventional tension. Notice how the delineated unconventional tensions are resolved in the following examples. (Ex. 6F)

Motives with TR

Using motives along with tension resolution gives the improvisor more leeway in sounding various colors of the chord and provides a greater sense of coherence and direction to the line. Here is an example of a single motive used over various chords. Take notice of which tensions are sounded in each of the examples. For more on this topic, please refer to the Motivic Playing chapter. (Ex. 6G)

Tension Resolution with other Improv Techniques

TR can be incorporated along with other improvisational techniques, such as Upper Structure Triads/7ths, Four Note Groupings and Triad/7th Pairs. Here are various examples that illustrate the application of those techniques along with TR. (Ex. 6H)

Sample TR lines over C Dom 7th

The following are possible lines over a C Dom 7 illustrating some of the techniques previously discussed. (Ex. 61)

Steps to Improvising on a Standard with Tensions

Create the Tension Line

Sketch out a tension line on a standard progression. In this next example, a tension line is created on the progression of a well-known standard *"All The Things You're Not"*. (Ex. 6J)

Resolve the Tension

Now sketch out the tension and the subsequent resolution of the tension to an adjacent chord tone. (Ex. 6K)

Add Syncopated Rhythms

Using only the tension and adjacent chord tone, create phrases with rhythmic syncopation. (Ex. 6L)

Additional Chord Tone

Lastly, add additional chord tones while making sure the tension resolution remains intact. (Ex. 6M)

Solo (Stella By Moonlight) with Tensions

Here is an example of a solo on a well-known standard. Every chord change uses one tension note to generate tension resolution. Play through the solo to determine which tensions were applied in each measure and where the points of resolution occur. (Ex. 6N)

Solo (None Of Me) with Chromatic Approach Notes & Tensions

We can combine the use of chromatic approach notes along with available tensions. The following solo on a well-known standard utilizes one non-chord tone per chord that is either a chromatic approach note or a tension. The chart before the solo lists which non-chord tones were used in the creation of the solo. This is a good way to practice improvising with TR. Pick a standard and predetermine which approach notes and tensions will be used along with chord tones to create lines through the progression. (Ex. 60)

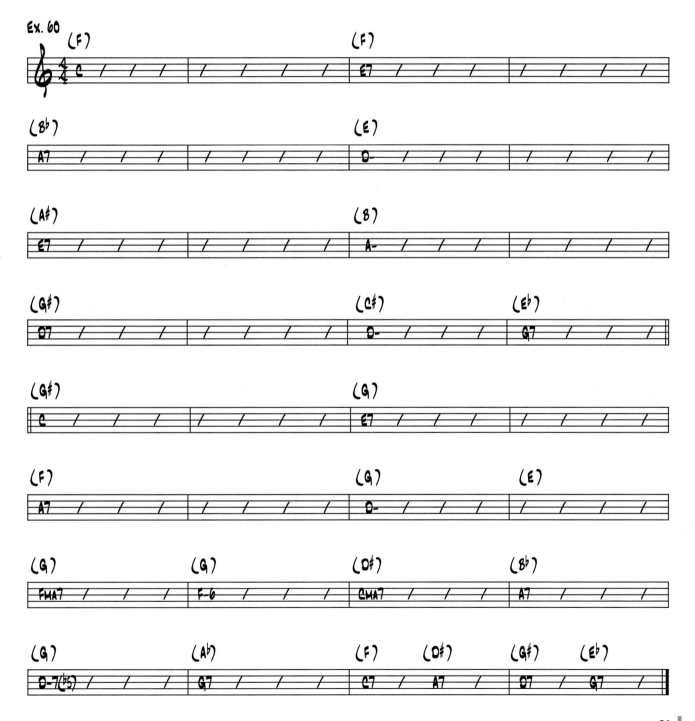

As evident by the many techniques addressed in this chapter, there are multiple ways to incorporate the concept of TR in one's improvisation. TR can create lines that are very simple and melodic or quite complex and pattern oriented. It is a very important and fundamental improvisational concept that can be applied in conjunction with many other concepts of improvisation.

Chord Scale Theory

The application of chord scales in improvisation is an important topic, since many improvisational techniques, such as Upper Structure Triads and 7th Chords, Four Note Groupings, Intervallic Playing and Pentatonics are chord scale based.

This chapter will address the many options of chord scales along with the criteria for choosing a specific scale over a chord. Conventional chord scale options listed according to chord types will be introduced first. The Advanced Chord Scale Theory section will discuss the employment of Cross-Referenced scales, Synthetic scales and Ethnic/Exotic scales. A variety of application techniques and ways of practicing chord scales will be addressed in the Chord Scale Application and Practices chapter.

Chord Scale Chart

The following chart contains the various chord scales that are available based upon specific chord types.

Major 7

Ionian	1 2 3 4 5 6 7
Ionian (#2)	1 #2 3 4 5 6 7
Lydian	1 2 3 #4 5 6 7
Lydian (#2)	1 #2 3 #4 5 6 7
Harmonic Major	1 2 3 4 5 b6 7

Major 7 #5

Lydian Augmented	1 2 3 #4 #5 6 7
Lydian Augmented (#2)	1 #2 3 #4 #5 6 7
Symmetrical Augmented	1 #2 3 5 #5 7
Symmetrical Augmented (#4)	1 #2 3 #4 5 #5 7
Bebop	1 2 3 4 5 #5 6 7
Ionian (#2) Bebop	1 #2 3 4 5 #5 6 7
Harmonic Major	1 2 3 4 5 b6 7

Minor 6

Melodic Minor	1 2 b3 4 5 6 7

Minor 7

Dorian	1 2 b3 4 5 6 b7
Aeolian	1 2 b3 4 5 b6 b7
Phrygian	1 b2 b3 4 5 b6 b7

Minor Major 7

Melodic Minor	1 2 b3 4 5 6 7
Harmonic Minor	1 2 b3 4 5 b6 7

Minor 7 b5

Locrian	1 b2 b3 4 b5 b6 b7
Locrian (natural 2)	1 2 b3 4 b5 b6 b7
Locrian (natural 2 & 6)	1 2 b3 4 b5 6 b7

Dominant 7

Mixolydian	1 2 3 4 5 6 b7
Mixolydian (b2, #2)	1 b2 #2 3 4 5 6 b7
Mixolydian (b6)	1 2 3 4 5 b6 b7
Lydian b7	1 2 3 #4 5 6 b7
Altered (with natural 4 & 5)	1 b2 #2 3 4 5 b6 b7
Altered (Diminished Whole Tone)	1 b2 #2 3 #4 (b5) b6 b7
Symmetrical Diminished (H/W)	1 b2 #2 3 #4 5 6 b7
Whole Tone	1 2 3 #4 (b5) #5 (b6) b7

Dominant 7 Sus 4

Mixolydian	1 2 3 4 5 6 b7
Mixolydian (b2, #2)	1 b2 #2 3 4 5 6 b7
Mixolydian (b6)	1 2 3 4 5 b6 b7
Altered (with natural 4 & 5)	1 b2 #2 3 4 5 b6 b7

Diminished 7

Symmetrical Diminished (W/H)	1 2 b3 4 b5 b6 6 7

The scales listed above are some of the many options that can be used for improvisation. The improvisor should have a solid grasp of these scales in all keys. In addition, the improvisor should also know which tensions are associated with each given chord scale. For example, a Lydian b7 scale on a Dom 7 will include tensions 9, #11 and 13.

Bebop Scales

The improvisor can also add a chromatic passing note to many of the above scales, thereby creating an eight-note scale. The theory behind the added chromatic note is that it allows the improvisor to sound chord tones on the downbeats and passing notes on the upbeats while playing 8th note based lines. Here are the options for adding the chromatic note:

For Maj 7 chords, add #5 (line will outline a Maj 6)
For Min 6 chords, add #5
For Dom 7/Dom 7 sus chords, add natural 7
For Min 7/Min 7 b5 chords, add natural 7

For example, C Lydian Bebop would be: 1 2 3 #4 5 #5 6 7
C Mixolydian Bebop would be: 1 2 3 4 5 6 b7 7

Choosing Chord Scales

When choosing a chord scale for a specific chord type, it is helpful to narrow down the important differences between each scale. For example, while both Ionian and Lydian scales can be applied to a Maj 7 chord, one contains a natural 4 and the other a #4. With that in mind, here is a chart that takes into account those scale differences in each chord type category.

Major 7

4 or #4?   2 or #2?

Minor 7

6 or b6?   If b6, 2 or b2?

Dominant 7

2 or b2, #2?   4 or #4?   6 or b6?

Minor 7 b5

2 or b2?   6 or b6?

Selecting chord scales can be very subjective and it is most often up to the improvisor to determine what colors may be sounded. For example, on a Min 7 chord, a Dorian scale will be brighter than a Phrygian scale. Many times, there is not a right or wrong choice. The improvisor may choose a different scale for the same chord on each successive chorus. Furthermore, multiple scales may be used for the duration of a single chord.

However, there are factors and specific criteria that should be addressed when choosing chord scales. One method is to select chord scales according to chord function. This works well for compositions with more conventional harmony, such as standards from the Great American Songbook, Jobim's Brazilian compositions, pop tunes, etc., where the general intent is to keep the chord scales diatonic to the overall tonality of the composition. Here are some examples for a major key tonality.

Diatonic Chord Function

I Maj 7	Ionian
II Min 7	Dorian
III Min 7	Phrygian
IV Maj 7	Lydian
V Dom 7	Mixolydian
VI Min 7	Aeolian
VII Min 7 b5	Locrian

Non-Diatonic Chord Function

V7 of V7	Lydian b7
Sub V7	Lydian b7
b II Maj 7	Lydian
b III Maj 7	Lydian
b VI Maj 7	Lydian
b VII Maj 7	Lydian
b VI Dom 7	Lydian b7
b VII Dom 7	Lydian b7
IV Min 6	Melodic Minor
# IV Min 7 b5	Locrian

The following criteria will be helpful in determining chord scales.

Since the improvisor is aware that the scale will contain the root, 3rd, 5th and 7th of the chord, the subsequent step is to determine appropriate passing notes. The following are three considerations to be made when choosing a chord scale for a given chord:

1. The Melody: If the melody includes a #4 on a Maj 7 chord, the most appropriate scale choice would be Lydian. Likewise, if the melody includes a b6 and a natural 2 on a Min 7 chord, the appropriate scale choice would be Aeolian. Please note: non-chord tones that classify as passing or approach notes, should not be used as a criteria in choosing a chord scale. Many times, the melody may not give any clues in determining the best chord scale choice.

2. The Previous Chord Scale: This is the most important factor in choosing the best chord scale. In essence, the intent is to retain as many notes as possible from one chord scale into the successive chord scale. For example, if a C-7 with an Aeolian scale precedes an Ab7 chord, the most likely scale choice for the Ab7 would be Ab Lydian b7. The reasoning would be as follows: C Aeolian scale contains the notes Bb, D and F, which are respectively scale degrees 2, #4 and 6 in Ab Lydian b7.

3. The Following Chord: This is an important criteria in choosing scales for a Dom 7 chord. A Dominant chord generally sets up the sound of the chord it resolves to, and is therefore influenced by it. A Dom 7 chord expected to go down a 5th to a Major type chord will take Mixolydian as first choice, but can also take Whole Tone, Symmetrical Diminished, Altered, etc., depending on the melody and/or context. A Dom 7 chord expected to go down a 5th to a Minor type chord will take a scale with a b13 and either a natural or altered 9, according to the chord symbol or context.

There can be many effective choices in the selection of chord scales for a given chord. The improvisor may at times choose atypical scales with the intent of sounding unconventional tensions. For example, a Lydian #2 scale can be used on a Maj 7 chord, thereby sounding tension #9. Similarly, a Locrian natural 2 and 6 scale can be used on a Min 7 b5 chord, thereby sounding tensions natural 9 and 13.

This discussion on choosing chord scales is only a general guideline. The improvisor is encouraged to experiment with all of the many scale options and experience their sound on a given chord in the context of a progression or composition.

Advanced Chord Scale Theory

The improvisor can deviate from conventional scale choice options by exploring additional chord scale options and techniques in the application of chord scales. Some of the possibilities include the use of Cross-Referenced, Synthetic, Hexatonic, and Ethnic/Exotic scales. Note: throughout all of the following examples, notice the tension emphasis in the lines.

Cross-Referencing Scales

A scale can be cross-referenced from one typical application and used on any other chord. Scalar runs and passages will often resolve tensions and/or chromatic notes as the lines proceed up or down. Consequently, the improvisor can select scales that ordinarily would not be thought of as typical scale choices for a given chord. This next example shows the application of a G Lydian scale over an F Maj 7 chord. Notice the resolution of the C# and F# as the line proceeds up the scale.
(Ex. 1A)

C Altered Bebop could be used over an Eb7 chord. This scale sounds both the 9 and b9. Scales that sound both the 9 and b9 or 13 and b13 can be effective scale choices. (Ex. 1B)

A Phrygian scale, normally used for a Min 7 chord, could also be applied over a Dom 7 sus chord, as illustrated in the following example. (Ex. 1C)

C Lydian b7 Bebop scale could be played over A7 sus. This application sounds the natural 9, b9 and #9. (Ex. 1D)

This next example cross-references a C Lydian b7 Bop scale over an E-7 b5 chord. (Ex. 1E)

A Sub V7 typically takes a Lydian b7 scale. However, as a deviation, a Lydian Augmented scale can be cross-referenced over the Sub V7 (Db7), consequently sounding tensions 9 and b13. (Ex. 1F)

A scale used on a V7 can also be cross-referenced and used on the related II Min 7. In the next example, the A Symmetrical Diminished scale used for the A7 chord is also applied to the E-7 b5 chord. (Ex. 1G)

A scale can be cross-referenced and applied to a variety of chords. Here is an example of a C Lydian #2 Bop scale used to create scalar lines over four measures. This example could be applied over the following chords: C Maj 7, D7, Eb7, F#-7 b5, F#7, G Maj 7, G Maj 7 #5, A-7, B7, B7 sus (Ex. 1H)

Harmonic Minor and Harmonic Major Scales

Due to their unique character, provided by a minor 3rd interval, both Harmonic Minor and Harmonic Major scales make interesting cross-referencing choices.

In order to better understand the Harmonic Minor scale, it is recommended that the improvisor explore its application over chords that are diatonic to the scale before attempting to cross-reference it over non-diatonic chords.

The C Harmonic Minor scale could be applied to the following diatonic chords:

C- Maj 7, D-7 b5, D°7, Eb Maj 7 #5, F-6, F-7, F-7 b5, F°7, G7, G7 sus, G+7, Ab6, Ab Maj 7, Ab-6, Ab- Maj 7, Ab°7, B°7

The following example illustrates a C Harmonic Minor scale utilized over an Ab Maj 7 chord (this scale can also be thought of as an Ab Lydian #2 scale). Note that the scale sounds the #9 over the Maj 7 chord. The #9 can be an interesting note, which the improvisor may choose to resolve, or not. (Ex. 2A)

The scale could also be used over a group of diatonic chords.
Below is a C Harmonic Minor scale applied over a II-7 b5 V7 I-6 in C Minor. (Ex. 2B)

The improvisor can subsequently cross-reference the Harmonic Minor scale over non-diatonic chords in order to generate lines that sound unusual tensions and passing/approach notes.

Here are some possible non-diatonic chords that C Harmonic Minor could be applied to:

C Maj 7, C-7, D7 sus, Eb Maj 7, F7, A-7 b5, A-7, A- Maj 7, Bb7, Bb7 sus, B7

The next example illustrates a C Harmonic Minor based pattern over an F7 chord. (Ex. 2C)

The following three examples of a Db Harmonic Minor scale played over A-6, C-7 and F-6, demonstrate how the improvisor can cross-reference the scale in order to obtain more dissonant notes or "avoid" notes over the underlying harmony. These interesting dissonances and unusual notes can then be resolved within notes of the cross-referenced scale, notes within a more conventional scale, or chord tones of the underlying chord. (Ex. 2D)

The scale could also be used over a group of non-diatonic chords. As previously mentioned, scales that sound both natural and altered tension notes can make for interesting lines over the underlying harmony.

In the following examples, make note of which conventional and unconventional tensions are sounded with each scale application, and how the tensions are resolved.

Below is a C Harmonic Minor scale applied over a V7 sus I6 in Eb. (Ex. 2E)

In the next example an Ab Harmonic Minor scale is applied over a II-7b5 V7 I-6 in C Minor. (Ex. 2F)

Lastly, a D Harmonic Minor scale is applied over a V7 sus I-6 in F Minor. (Ex. 2G)

As with the Harmonic Minor scale, it is recommended that the improvisor explore the application of the Harmonic Major over chords that are diatonic to the scale before attempting to cross-reference it over non-diatonic chords.

The C Harmonic Major scale could be applied to the following diatonic chords:

C Maj 7, C Maj 7 #5, D-7 b5, D°7, E-7, E7, F-6, F- Maj 7, F°7, G7, G7 sus, Ab Maj 7 #5, Ab°7, B°7

The next example illustrates a C Harmonic Major scale applied over an F-6 chord. (Ex. 2H)

The scale could also be used over a group of diatonic chords.
This example applies the C Harmonic Major scale to a II-7 b5 V7 I in C. (Ex. 2I)

The improvisor can subsequently cross-reference the scale over non-diatonic chords in order to generate lines that sound unusual tensions and passing/approach notes.

Possible non-diatonic chords that the C Harmonic Major scale could be applied to include:

D-6, D7 sus, E7 sus, F Maj 7, F-7, Ab6, Ab-6, A-7, A- Maj 7, Bb7, B7 sus

This example shows a C Harmonic Major scale used over a Bb7 chord. (Ex. 2J)

The following three examples of a Db Harmonic Major scale played over Ab-7, D7 and G-7 b5, demonstrate how the improvisor can cross-reference the scale in order to obtain more dissonant notes or "avoid" notes over the underlying harmony. These interesting dissonances and unusual notes can then be resolved within notes of the cross-referenced scale, notes within a more conventional scale, or chord tones of the underlying chord. (Ex. 2K)

The scale could also be used over a group of non-diatonic chords. The following three examples illustrate various cross-referenced applications of the Harmonic Major scale.

Here is an Eb Harmonic Major scale utilized over a II-7 b5 V7 sus I-6 in C Minor. (Ex. 2L)

C Harmonic Major scale can be used over a II-7 V7 I in Eb. This scale application sounds more unorthodox tensions. Notice how the application of pattern based tension resolution contributes to the strength of the line. (Ex. 2M)

Here is a D Harmonic Major applied over a II-7 V7 I in F. (Ex. 2N)

Synthetic Chord Scales

Synthetic scales can be applied over a variety of chord types or groups of chords. Here are two synthetic scales that contain two minor 3rd intervals. The inclusion of the minor 3rd intervals in the scale can lend character and interest to the improvised line, allowing the improvisor to sound unusual notes and colors over the underlying harmony.

Double Harmonic Major   1 b2 3 4 5 b6 7

C Double Harmonic Major could be applied to the following chords:

C Maj 7, C Maj 7 #5, D-7 b5, D°7, Db Maj 7, Eb7, Eb7 sus, E7, F- Maj 7, G7, G7 sus, Ab Maj 6, Ab Maj 7 #5, A Maj 7, A Maj 7 #5, A-7, A- Maj 7, Bb7, Bb-7, B7 sus

Synthetic chord scales can also be played over groups of chords. Here is a C Double Harmonic Major scale used over a II-7 V7 I V7/II-7 in C. (Ex. 3A)

This is an example of C Double Harmonic Major applied to a II-7 b5 V7 I-6 in A Minor. (Ex. 3B)

Double Harmonic Minor   1 2 b3 #4 5 b6 7

C Double Harmonic Minor scale (which contains the same notes as G Double Harmonic Major scale) can be applied to the following chords:

C Maj 7, C Maj 7 #5, C- Maj 7, D7, D7 sus, Eb6, Eb Maj 7 #5, F7, G7, G7 sus, Ab Maj 7, Ab7, A°7, A-7 b5, A- Maj 7, Bb7, Bb7 sus, B7

Below is an example of C Double Harmonic Minor applied to a II-7b5 V7 I-6 in G Minor. (Ex. 3C)

This is another example of the same scale application over the same progression. (Ex. 3D)

Here is a G Double Harmonic Minor utilized over the same progression. (Ex. 3E)

Combining Both Double Harmonic Scales

The following example utilizes both G Double Harmonic Major and G Double Harmonic Minor scales on a II-7 V7 I cadence in Bb. Notice how the application of these two scales creates a unified sounding line, while bringing out interesting passing/approach notes and unusual tensions. (Ex. 3F)

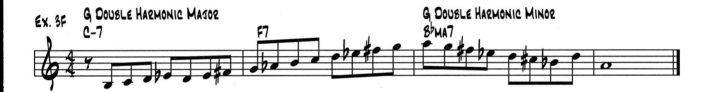

Here is an example that employs both a G Double Harmonic Minor and C Double Harmonic Major scales over a V7 chord. Notice the color variation in the line from one measure to the next as the chord scales change. (Ex. 3G)

Motives from Double Harmonic Scales

The improvisor can experiment with the sound of the characteristic minor 3rd and 1/2 step intervals found in these scales. The structural strength of these motives can be the basis for interesting and rich sounding lines.

In the following example, the scale-derived motive is comprised of a minor 3rd, 1/2 step and 1/2 step. The motive can be transposed to other points over the chord. (Ex. 3H)

This next example utilizes another scalar motive comprised of a 1/2 step, minor 3rd and 1/2 step. The motive is then transposed to other points over the chord. (Ex. 3I)

Combining the motive along with its transposition can create interesting scalar possibilities. Here is an interesting scale that illustrates the technique and its application on C7. Notice the tensions include 9, b9, 13 and b13. (Ex. 3J)

Symmetrical Tritonic Scale

In addition to the Symmetrical Diminished and Symmetrical Augmented scales, there is the Symmetrical Tritonic scale. This scale is based upon the division of the octave into three equidistant parts.

The three points of the scale's equidistant division are the basis for the creation of the three identical scalar fragments. The following is an example of the concept along with its application over several Dom 7 chords. (Ex. 3K)

Here is another example utilizing the same points of the scale's division, except with different scalar fragments. (Ex. 3L)

Hexatonic Scales

Hexatonic scales are six-note scales created from Triad Pairs. Here is an example that applies a C-/Db- Hexatonic scale on a Gb7 chord. In this case, the Gb7 is functioning as a bVII Dom 7, which would ordinarily take a Lydian b7 scale. However, the C-/Db- Hexatonic scale sounds both the 9 and b9, as well as the #11 and 13, proving to be an effective choice. This line could also be applied over many other chords, including C7, Eb7, Bb-7, Bb-7 b5, Db Maj 7 and Db- Maj 7. For more on Hexatonic scales, please refer to the chapter on Triad Pairs. (Ex. 3M)

Ethnic & Exotic Scales

There are scales from many cultures throughout the world that can be utilized to create interesting lines over a variety of chords.

Here are some of the many scales that the improvisor can utilize:

Neapolitan scale:	1 b2 b3 4 5 6 7
Neapolitan Minor scale:	1 b2 b3 4 5 b6 7
Japanese scale:	1 b2 4 6 b7
Oriental scale:	1 b2 3 4 b5 6 b7

The following are examples of the above listed scales in the key of C along with corresponding chord applications. (Ex. 4A)

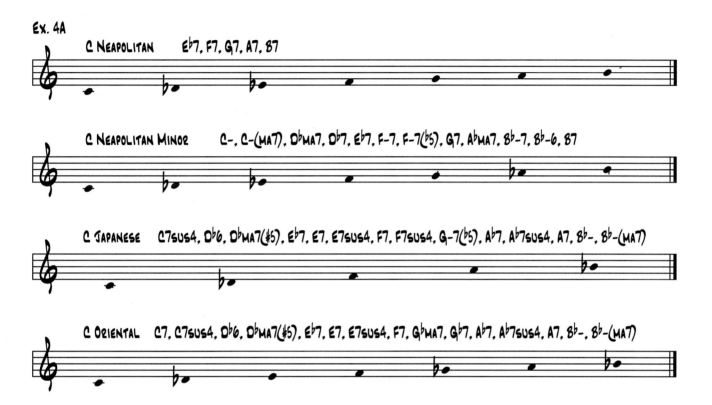

Ex. 4A

C Neapolitan   E♭7, F7, G7, A7, B7

C Neapolitan Minor   C-, C-(MA7), D♭MA7, D♭7, E♭7, F-7, F-7(♭5), G7, A♭MA7, B♭-7, B♭-6, B7

C Japanese   C7sus4, D♭6, D♭MA7(#5), E♭7, E7, E7sus4, F7, F7sus4, G-7(♭5), A♭7, A♭7sus4, A7, B♭-, B♭-(MA7)

C Oriental   C7, C7sus4, D♭6, D♭MA7(#5), E♭7, E7, E7sus4, F7, G♭MA7, G♭7, A♭7, A♭7sus4, A7, B♭-, B♭-(MA7)

Many of the ethnic and exotic scales may also be known as other existing modes/scales, or as a mode derived from a scale or Pentatonic scale. Below are some examples:

Algerian or Egyptian scale: 1 2 b3 #4 5 b6 7 (Double Harmonic Minor)
Byzantine or Persian scale: 1 b2 3 4 5 b6 7 (Double Harmonic Major)
Japanese scale: 1 b2 b3 4 5 b6 b7 (Phrygian)
Arabian scale: 1 b2 b3 4 b5 b6 b7 (Locrian)
Hebrew or Jewish scale: 1 b2 3 4 5 b6 b7
Ake Bono (Japanese):   1 2 b3 5 b6
Kumoi (Japanese):   1 b2 4 5 b6
In Sen (Japanese):   1 b2 4 5 b7
Hon-Kumoi-Joshi (Japanese):   1 b2 4 #5 b7
Iwato Scale (Japanese):   1 b2 4 b5 b7

Here are examples of Ethnic/Exotic scales applied to typical progressions. (Ex. 4B-4D)

Creating New Scales

The improvisor can create scales by adding chromatic notes and/or leaving out notes in an existing scale. Here are some considerations in the process of creating new scales.

Adding Notes

When adding notes to an existing scale, consider selecting an interesting tension or approach note and evaluate how the tension/approach note will be resolved to an adjacent chord tone or scale note. (Ex. 5A)

Leaving Out Notes

Omitting notes in the scale can increase the focus on more unusual notes over the underlying chord. However, merely leaving out notes may not prove to be effective, unless a unique interval (such as a minor 3rd) is established and the scale contains unusual approach notes and/or unconventional tensions. (Ex. 5B)

The omission of additional scale notes can reveal interesting intervals (such as a tritone), creating more angularity and openness in the lines. It can also result in interesting Pentatonic scales. (Ex. 5C)

Knowledge of chord scales along with skillful and musical application ability is an important asset for the improvisor to have. As previously mentioned, the implementation of many other improvisational techniques relies upon the improvisor's command of chord scales.

Chord Scale Application and Practices

The application of chord scales is an important facet of improvisation. While it is important to have good knowledge of chord scales, the way they are applied is also crucial in effective improvisation. Too often, improvised solos sound as though the soloist runs up and down scales randomly. This chapter will first address ways of practicing scales, which in turn will enable the improvisor to better handle the great variety of chord scale application techniques conveyed thereafter.

Practice Routines

Visualizing The Scale

When learning a new scale, play it up and down the entire range of the instrument. Continue by playing random notes up and down the entire range and sporadically jumping octaves.

Playing Scale from Every Scale Degree

Playing the scale from every scale degree can be a good learning routine when dealing with new scales. The following example shows a C7 Altered scale starting on Gb and played from every scale degree up an octave. When utilizing this routine, it is beneficial to take notice of how the scale sounds from the various starting points. For example, C Altered played from Gb becomes a Gb Lydian b7 scale. Make sure to follow this process for every scale degree. (Ex. 1A)

Playing Scale from Designated Starting Points

As a variation, the scale can be played from designated points within the scale. This next example illustrates the scale executed from C to E to Ab (up in major 3rds). (Ex. 1B)

The following example employs the same designated starting points, but only uses six notes of the scale. The improvisor may also experiment with four or five notes. (Ex. 1C)

In this example the designated starting points descend in perfect 4th intervals through the scale. (Ex. 1D)

This example features the same starting points, but now using only five notes of the scale. (Ex. 1E)

Ascending and Descending 7th Arpeggios

Playing diatonic 7th chords from every scale degree is another good practice routine to become fluid with chord scales. It is also beneficial to take note of which chords are sounded as they move up and down the scale. The following example sounds C-7 b5, Db- Maj 7, Eb-7, E Maj 7 #5, Gb7, etc. (Ex. 1F)

Ascending and Descending Combination

Ascending and descending arpeggios can be alternated as they proceed down through the scale. (Ex. 1G)

Combining Arpeggios with Scalar Phrases

This next example illustrates ascending diatonic 7th arpeggios connected with descending scalar segments. (Ex. 1H)

Here is the reverse of the example above. (Ex. 1I)

Simple Scalar Patterns

In working with a scale, it can also be beneficial to play simple scalar patterns that move through the scale. Here is a simple descending four-note scalar pattern. (Ex. 1J)

This is the pattern from the previous example moving down in 3rds through the scale. (Ex. 1K)

Here is an ascending/descending combination of the same pattern. (Ex. 1L)

This is another variation. Notice that the combination of the ascending and descending scalar pattern only sounds five notes of the scale. The pattern can be sounded at various points in the scale. (Ex. 1M)

Simple Scalar Patterns with a Skip

Using a skip can open up additional possibilities. Here is a four-note pattern that includes a skip. The pattern is played from every scale degree. (Ex. 1N)

The following is a six-note pattern that begins with a skip. The example is written as 8th notes in 3/4, but the pattern could be played in triplets or 16th notes in 4/4. Executing the pattern as 16th notes would create an interesting sense of phrasing. (Ex. 1O)

Here is another pattern related to the one above. (Ex. 1P)

Chord Scale Application

This section will address some techniques and devices that relate to the application of chord scales, some of which were previously discussed in the Chord Scale Theory chapter.

Some of the practices hereafter illustrated, which can enhance the application of chord scales include deleting and/or adding notes in the scalar passage, use of unexpected leaps, changes in the direction of the line and use of space and syncopated rhythms. Other important elements that will also be exemplified are the use of motives and patterns.

Deleting Notes/Change in Direction of the Line

Playing note for note scales up and down one's instrument can sound as though an academic exercise. More musical results can be achieved by simply leaving out a note or two in the execution of a chord scale and by changing the direction of the improvised line.

The following example applies an Eb Lydian b7 scale to an Eb7 chord. The interest and unpredictability in the line is obtained by the omission of notes along with the change in the direction of the line. Also, take note of two other important elements employed in this next example:
(Ex. 2A)

- Emphasized tension on the underlying chord by placing non chord tones on strong beats

- Resolution of tensions to chord tones

For more on tensions and tension resolution, please refer to the Tension Resolution chapter.

Here is another example that applies a G Altered scale to a G Dom 7 chord. Again, notice the deletion of notes and the strong emphasis of tension notes over the underlying chord. (Ex. 2B)

Adding Chromatic Notes

In addition to deleting notes, adding chromatic passing or approach notes can also be effective in making the scalar passage or run sound less formulaic. The use of chromatic passing and approach notes allows the line to deviate from the tonal center of the underlying chord and progression.

Most often, improvisors choose very conventional scales, which can at times be acceptable. However, adhering to only using the notes of diatonic scales can result in lines that are quite bland and uninteresting.

This next example uses a G Altered scale along with chromatic passing notes as applied to a G7 chord. (Ex. 3A)

The following three examples illustrate how adding one or two out of scale notes can have a strong impact on the improvised line. The line is built with an Eb Locrian natural 2 scale over the Eb-7 b5. The first example uses only diatonic notes. (Ex. 3B)

In this example, one of the notes is replaced with an out of scale chromatic approach note. The non-diatonic note (the major 7th of the underlying chord) is sounded on the 3rd beat of the measure and is subsequently resolved to the root of the chord. (Ex. 3C)

Lastly, one more diatonic note is replaced with a non-diatonic note that sounds the natural 6th of the underlying chord. (Ex. 3D)

In all three previous examples, the scalar pattern remained unchanged. However, notice how the replacement of diatonic notes with out of scale approach notes impacted the line.

Here is another example that illustrates the application of three out of scale notes in a line over Db Maj 7. (Ex. 3E)

The out of scale notes in this next example are chromatic passing notes. (Ex. 3F)

The following example uses a Db Harmonic Minor scale with an added chromatic passing note. Notice how the line sounds an Ab7 US7th chord over the C7. The pattern is repeated down an octave. (Ex. 3G)

The out of scale notes in this last example are chromatic passing and approach notes. (Ex. 3H)

Using Space & Syncopation

Use of space and syncopation can be a simple solution to making a scalar passage or run sound more musical. This next example applies an Ab Lydian b7 scale to an Ab7 chord with triplet based syncopated rhythmic figures. Notice how by being placed on the strong beats tension notes are emphasized. (Ex. 4)

Techniques Applied to a Scale

The following examples illustrate some of the musical devices previously addressed as applied to an Ab Lydian b7 scale over an Ab7 chord. (Ex. 5A - Ex. 5F)

Note Deletion: (Ex. 5A)

Added Chromatic Notes: (Ex. 5B)

Note Deletion/Added Chromatic Passing Notes: (Ex. 5C)

Change in Direction of the Line: (Ex. 5D)

Use of Space: (Ex. 5E)

Use of Syncopation: (Ex. 5F)

Changing Scales

Different combinations of scales can be used in runs and scalar passages on one individual chord. This next example utilizes an Ab Lydian b7 scale in the first measure and an Ab Altered natural 4 & 5 scale in the second measure. (Ex. 6A)

The example below uses an F Lydian b7 scale for the first two beats of the measure and an F Symmetrical Diminished (H/W) for the last two beats over the F7 chord. (Ex. 6B)

Breaking Down the Scale into Two Groups

This scalar concept takes a scale and divides it up into two groups of notes. In the following example, an A Lydian b7 scale applied to an A7 chord is divided into a four-note group and a three-note group. (Ex. 7A)

The above scale is now played in 8th note triplets, reflecting the four-note and three-note groups in various inversions throughout the line. (Ex. 7B)

The improvisor should experiment with other scales as well as with different note-groups variations.

Utilizing Motives/Patterns

As previously mentioned, the improvisor should avoid randomly playing scales up and down the instrument as a means of creating lines. One technique that can help in this regard is the implementation of patterns and motives to chord scales. The use of motives and scalar patterns can greatly enhance the character of the line. The transposition of motives to various points in a scale´ results in the establishment of patterns.

The following example illustrates the use of a motive that is transposed to various points in the scale. The scales used in the example are D Locrian natural 2 (D-7 b5) and G Altered (G7). (Ex. 8A)

Here is an example that illustrates the use of multiple motives. The following scales were used in the example: G Locrian natural 2 along with a chromatic approach note (G-7 b5), C (H/W) Symmetrical Diminished (C7), F Melodic Minor (F-6) and D Altered (D7). Notice how the placement of tension notes on the downbeats emphasizes their function over the underlying chords. (Ex. 8B)

Dom 7th Patterns

With the great variety of scale options available for Dom 7 chords, there are many possible patterns and scalar motives that the improvisor can experiment with. Here are some of the numerous possibilities.

This next example illustrates a scalar pattern (based upon C Altered on C7) played from every scale degree. The pattern could be applied to countless other scales. (Ex. 9A)

Here is a pattern (also using a C Altered scale over C7) that descends in major 3rd intervals and outlines an Ab+ triad. (Ex. 9B)

As previously demonstrated, Harmonic Minor scales can be very effective over Dom 7 chords. The next three examples illustrate pattern-based lines featuring a Db Harmonic Minor scale over C7. Notice that the scale sounds both tensions 13 and b13, which can be a compelling sound. (Ex. 9C)

This next example illustrates a seven-note pattern that is repeated down an octave. (Ex. 9D)

Here the pattern is comprised of two four-note groups. Notice how beats 3 and 4 use the same notes as beats 1 and 2, but in a different order. (Ex. 9E)

Patterns with Chromatic Notes

As it was previously addressed, the use of chromatic notes can be an important technique in the application of scales. The next example features a C Altered natural 4 and 5 scale with chromatic passing notes. Notice how the initial notes of each two beat pattern outline a Diminished chord. (Ex. 10A)

This last example illustrates the use of several patterns created from a D Altered scale over a D7 chord. Notice the use of chromatic passing and approach notes. (Ex. 10B)

For more on the topic of motives/patterns, please refer to the Motivic Playing chapter.

The application of chord scales in improvisation is an expansive subject that the improvisor should explore. Many of the important improvisational concepts are based on the application of chord scales. Consequently, the improvisor should have a fundamental grasp on the use and application of chord scales for improvisation. It is suggested that the improvisor begin with more conventional scales and gradually incorporate more unconventional scales thereafter.

Harmonic Practices

A comprehensive and in-depth knowledge of jazz harmony is indispensable to the improvisor. Many improvisational concepts are based on harmonic principles that allow the improvisor to deviate from the original underlying harmony of a standard song progression. The application of harmonic principles as a means of creating lines affords the improvisor to create chromatic melodic ideas with a strong sense of logic and direction. Musicians such as innovator/sax player John Coltrane and pianists, such as Herbie Hancock and Chick Corea, have utilized advanced harmonic techniques in their lines. Coltrane exploited his "sheets of sound" and advanced superimposed harmony. Hancock and Corea achieved highly intriguing lines through their choices of harmonic deviations.

The utilization of harmonic techniques is not relegated to the players of today. Sax players like Coleman Hawkins and Don Byas were using reharmonization and substitution methods in their solos. Pianist Art Tatum was a master with harmony, substitutions and reharmonization techniques. Within the language of Bebop, players like Charlie Parker and Sonny Stitt were using a variety of harmonic devices on a consistent basis in their solos. Contemporary sax players such as Dave Liebman, Michael Brecker and Bob Berg have incorporated many harmonic techniques that have resulted in unique and interesting chromatic lines.

There are many concepts, techniques and topics on the study of jazz harmony, as well as many books that address the subject. However, in this chapter we will limit our scope of jazz harmony to specific approaches and concepts that can be applied to improvisation.

The improvisor is encouraged to experiment with creating lines based upon the harmonic concepts and devices discussed in this section. In doing so, an effort should be made to convey the new change(s) as clearly as possible. While improvisational techniques such as Pentatonics, Triad Pairs and Four Note Groupings can be incorporated along with these harmonic concepts, it can be more effective to simply outline the new change(s), since the harmonic deviation is the important aspect of the line. Bringing out guide tone lines can also be effective in sounding the new change(s).

For ease of layout and clarity in addressing the concepts, sample musical examples will be included at the end of the section.

II-7 V7 Reharmonization Techniques

The following examples illustrate the various chord substitutions that are possible on a standard II-7 V7 in the key of C.

Sub V7

A common device is to use a Substitute V7 (known as a Sub V7 or Tritone Sub) for the G7.

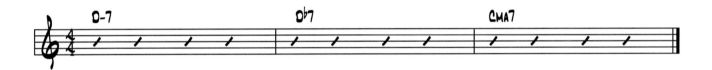

The related II-7 of the Sub V7 can also be used along with the Sub V7 in place of the G7.

The related II-7 of the Sub V7 can replace part of the D-7.

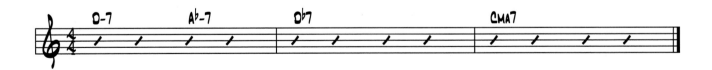

The related II-7 of the Sub V7 can replace the D-7 altogether.

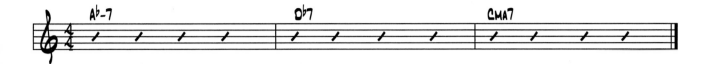

Diminished Based Reharmonization of V7

By associating G7 b9 to a Diminished chord (Ab°7) and consequently to the related Symmetrical Diminished scale, it becomes apparent that G7 b9, Bb7 b9, Db7 b9 and E7 b9 are all chord structures found in the scale. Therefore, any of these Dom 7 chords (along with their related II-7s) can substitute in place of the G7 or D-7 G7.

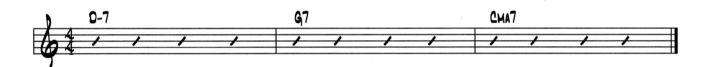

Using one of the Dom 7 substitutions in place of the G7.

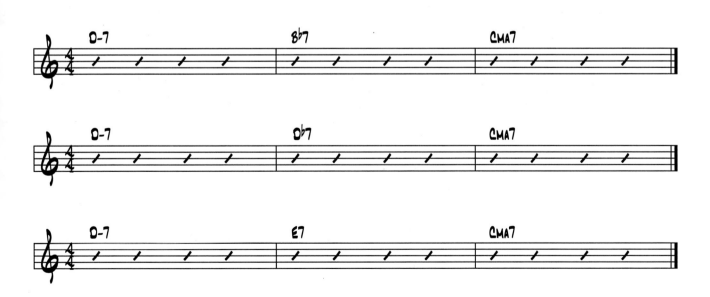

Combining the use of two Dom 7 chords in place of the G7.

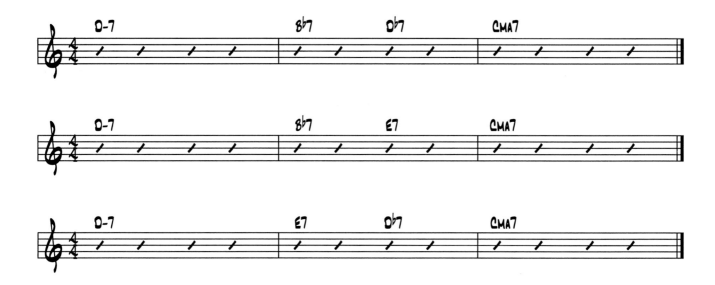

Using all three Dom 7 substitutions.

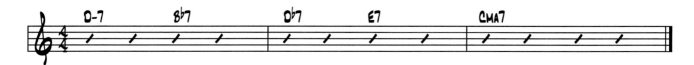

The Dom 7 substitutions along with their related II-7s can be utilized in place of the G7.

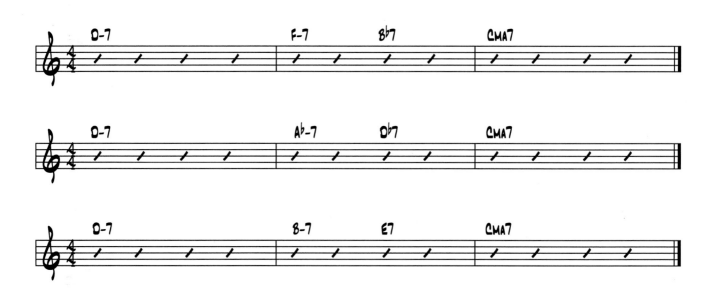

The related II-7s and Dom 7 substitutions can be used in place of the D-7 G7.

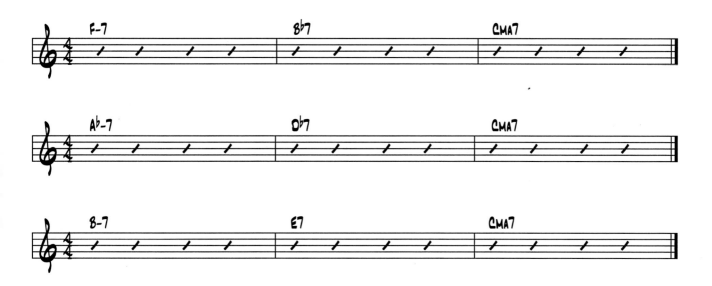

The combination of only the related II-7s of the substitute Dom 7 the along with the original II-7 is also possible.

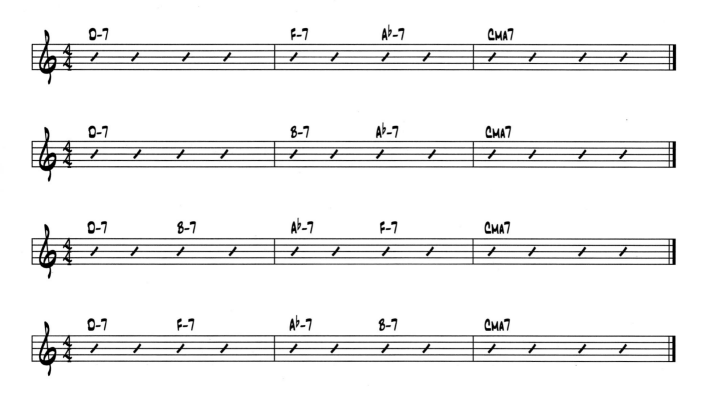

Diminished Based Reharmonization of I Dim 7

The V7 (G7) can be replaced with a I Dim 7 as an approach chord to the I Maj.

The four related Dom 7 b9 chords along with their related II-7s can then substitute for the
I Dim 7 chord. For example in the key of C: C Dim 7 is the same as B7 b9, D7 b9, F7 b9 and Ab7 b9.
Here is the application of this concept for a II-7 V7 I in the key of C.

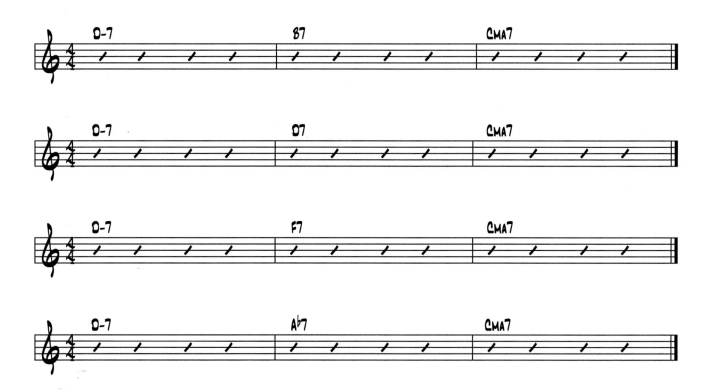

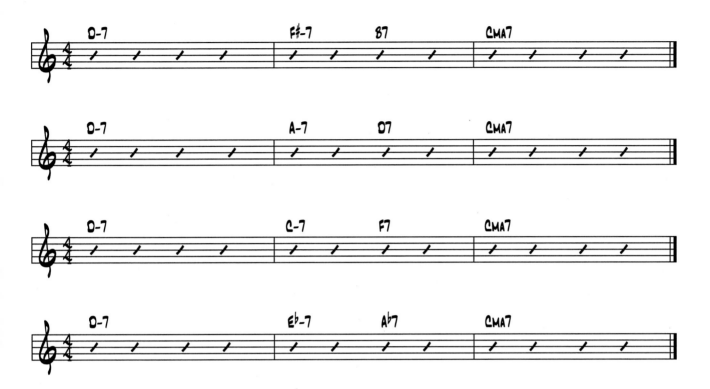

Secondary Dominant – V7 of V7

The II-7 can be replaced with a V7 of V7.

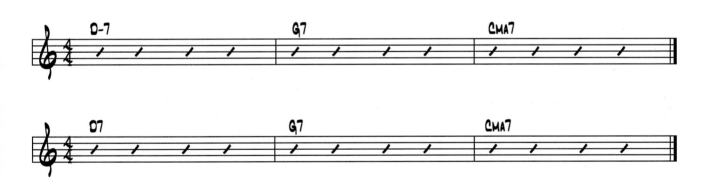

The related II-7 of the V7 of V7 can also be used along with the V7 of V7.

A Sub V7 can be utilized in place of the V7 of V7.

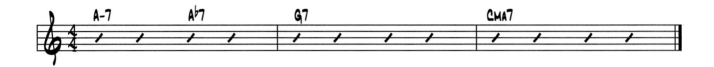

The related II-7 of the Sub V7 can be included.

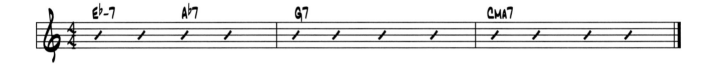

The related II-7 of the Sub V7 and the original II-7 V7 may be integrated (also known as Chromatic II-7 V7).

The Sub V7 and its related II-7 can be combined with the Sub V7 of I.

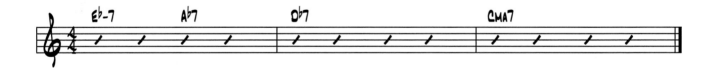

The related II-7 of the Sub V7 of I may also be included.

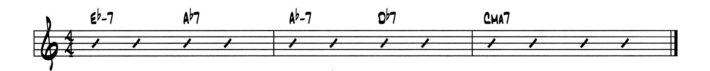

The related II-7 of the Sub V7 of I may be used by itself.

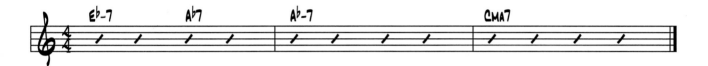

The related II-7 of the Sub V7 of V7 may also be used by itself.

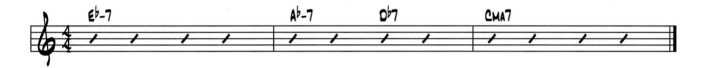

Both the related II-7 of the Sub V7 of V7 and Sub V7 of I can be used by themselves.

The related II-7 of the Sub V7 of V7 and the original V7 can be combined.

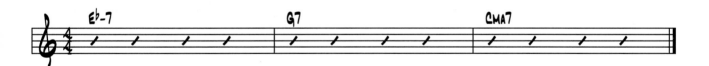

These are some of the many possible variations available over a standard II-7 V7. The improvisor should try using these variations to create lines over a standard II-7 V7 as well as to explore other alternative harmonic variations.

Modal Interchange Chord Substitution

Modal Interchange Chords are those that are borrowed from a parallel tonality for use in the primary tonality. Many of the common modal interchange chords originate from the parallel Natural Minor tonality. Other common parallel scale applications include Melodic Minor, Dorian and Phrygian. Possible Modal Interchange Chords include: b II Maj 7, II-7 b5, b III Maj 7, IV-6, IV- Maj 7, IV-7, V-7, b VI Maj 7, b VI7, b VII Maj 7, b VII7 and b VII7 sus.

The chords can substitute for the II-7, the V7 or II-7 V7 in a II-7 V7 I Maj progression. Here are some examples illustrating this concept:

Replacing the V7.

Replacing the II-7.

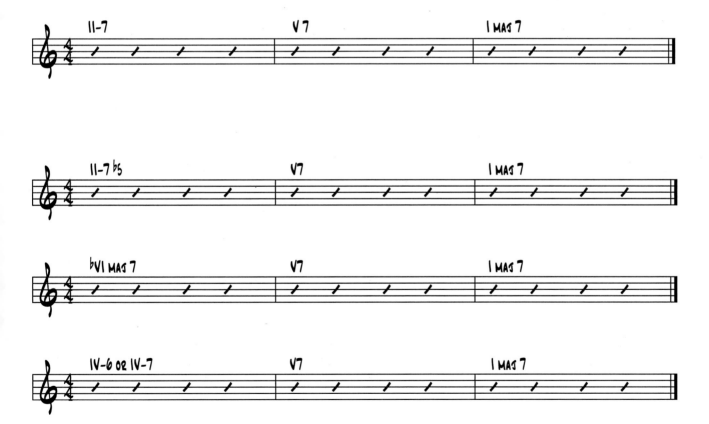

Replacing the II-7 V7.

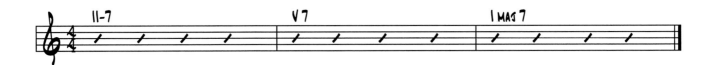

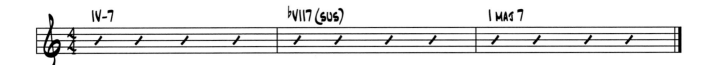

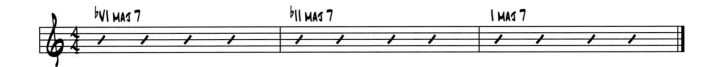

Harmonic Generalization

This concept isolates the essence of the harmonic intent of a specific combination of chords and reduces the amount of chord structures while retaining the primary cadential intent. Certain chords such as related II-7s, passing diatonic and passing Diminished chords can be omitted with this process.

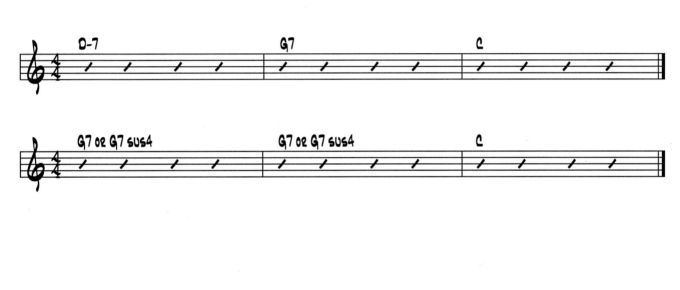

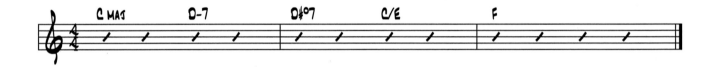

Use of V7, Sub V7 and Related II-7s

Any chord can be preceded by a V7 or Sub V7 along with the related II-7 chord. Here are some examples illustrating this concept.

V7 b9 Alternation

A chord can be alternated with its own V7 b9 (or Dim 7 a 1/2 step below) in order to create the effect of tension resolution and a sense of harmonic movement over the underlying chord structure. The V7 b9 should be resolved to the target chord. Here is an example on a Min 7 chord.

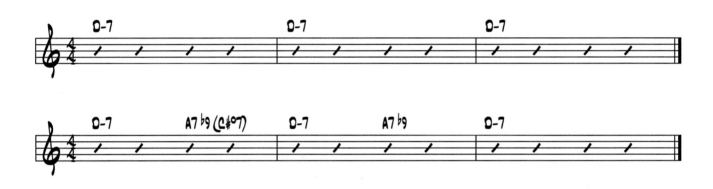

Here is an example on a Dom 7 sus chord.

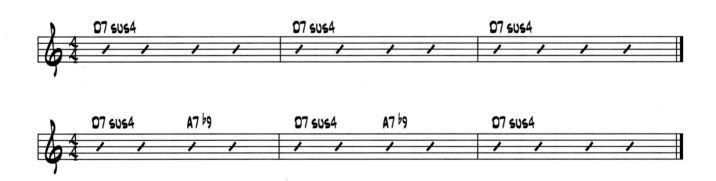

Approach Chords

A chord can be preceded by an approach chord (triad or 7th chord) that creates harmonic tension over the underlying harmony. The approach chord can occur during the beginning of the measure of the target chord or before, in the previous measure. It is important that the approach chord be smoothly resolved into the target chord. Here are examples of possible approach chords.

Here are some examples for a C Maj 7 chord.

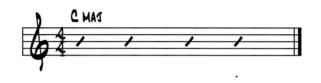

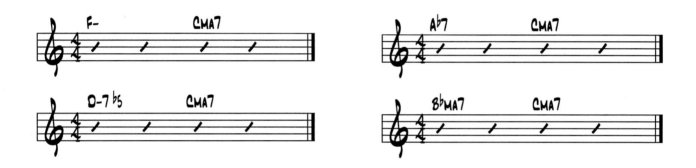

Diatonic and Chromatic Passing Chords

Improvised lines can outline diatonic, passing Diminished and chromatic approach triads or 7th chords over the underlying chord change. The lines should move quickly through each change as they weave through the passing chords. Here are some examples for Dom 7th chords.

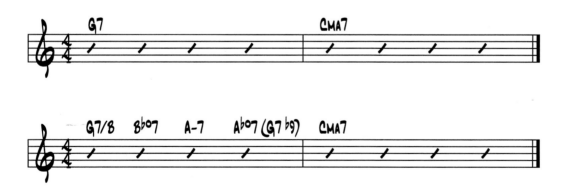

Turnaround Variations

There are many turnaround variations that the improvisor can utilize. Different variations can be used from chorus to chorus on a standard tune progression. Here are some of the many possibilities in the key of C.

There are many more possible turnaround variations. The improvisor is encouraged to explore other combinations as well as to listen to recordings for ideas on turnarounds.

Use of Chromatic Lines

Chromatic lines moving in the chord can help create a sense of motion and direction in the line. Here are some possible common lines.

Maj 7   (scale degrees 5 to #5 to 6)
Min 7   (scale degrees 1 to 7 to b7 to 6)
Min 6   (scale degrees 5 to #5 to 6)

Chord Alteration

Improvisors can alter a chord without necessarily changing the basic chord quality and harmonic function. Here are some viable alterations.

Maj 7 to Maj 7 #5 (can be resolved back to Maj 7 or Maj 6 if desired)
Maj 7 to Dim Maj 7 (can be resolved back to Maj 7 if desired)
Min 7 to Min 6, Min 7 b5, Min Maj 7 or Dim Maj 7
Min 7 b5 to Dim Maj 7
Dom 7 to Dom 7 sus, Dom 7 sus b9, 13 or Dom 7 sus altered

Harmonic Displacement

This technique retains the original chords. However, the chords can be anticipated or delayed. These are several examples illustrating the use of this concept.

Superimposition

This technique involves the superimposition of other chords and progressions over the underlying chord(s). The outlining of the superimposed structures gives the lines unity and a sense of direction, while creating varying degrees of dissonance over the underlying harmony. Here are some options of superimposition.

Extended Dominants

Extended Dominants can be used in place of the original harmony. Once a target chord is established, the improvisor can "backcycle" with extended Dominants from the target chord. When creating lines with the extended Dominants, consider bringing out the guide tone lines of the Dominant chords and try to connect each Dominant via stepwise motion. Here are a few examples.

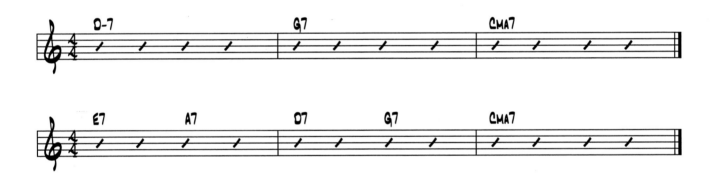

Blues (first 4 bars):

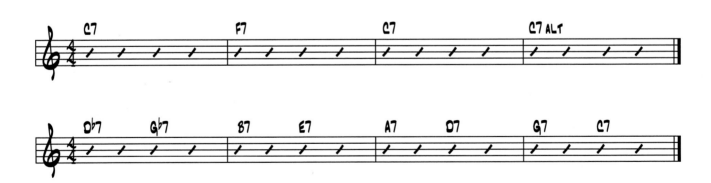

Rhythm Changes (first 4 bars):

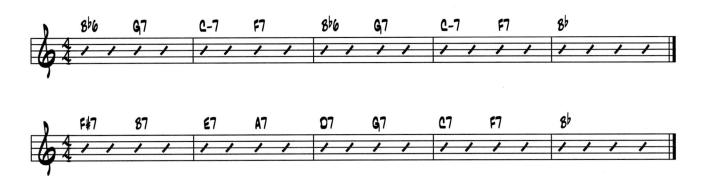

3 Tonic System

Many improvisors have used Coltrane's concept of playing in tonal centers major 3rds apart. Coltrane applied the concept to some of his compositions, such as Giant Steps and Countdown (based on the changes of Tune Up). He also applied the concept to many standards including the Gershwin classic But Not For Me. The following example illustrates the concept as applied to a II-7 V7 I Maj 7 in the key of C:

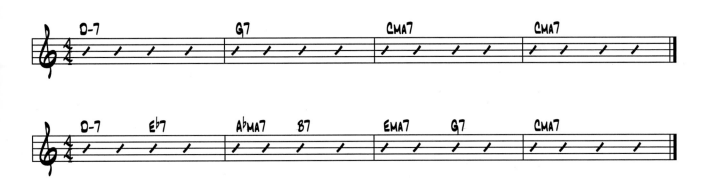

Other variations:

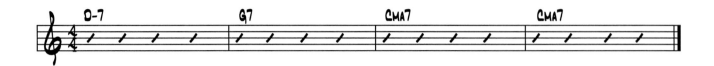

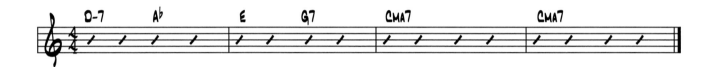

Parallel Tonal Substitution

The original progression can be replaced with chords of the same harmonic function transposed to another key. For example, a II-7 V7 I Maj 7 in C would be replaced with a II-7 V7 I Maj 7 in a new key.

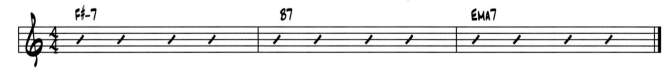

V7 or II-7 V7 Superimposition

Sax player Dave Liebman uses this technique in his lines. This method is conducive to creating chromatic lines that have a strong sense of direction and can weave in and out of the changes. The concept involves producing lines based upon superimposed V7 or II-7 V7 chords over the underlying harmony.

Lines based upon the V7 or II-7 V7 chord structures have an inherent sense of flow and direction and should resolve clearly and smoothly into the target chord. Moreover, the use of diatonic and chromatic approach notes in conjunction with the outlining of the superimposed chords can help create Bebop type lines with a contemporary flavor. The skillful use of this technique can be effective in increasing the degree of tension in one's overall playing. Here are some examples in the key of C.

The superimposed chord selection can include a series of V7 chords or II-7 V7s based upon a specific interval or pattern.

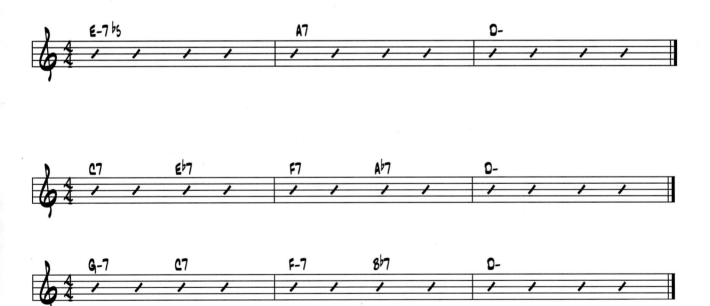

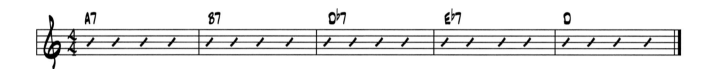

The superimposed chord selection may instead utilize a random combination of V7s or II-7 V7s.

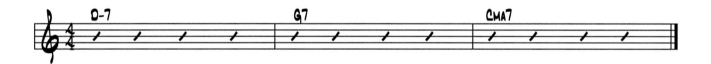

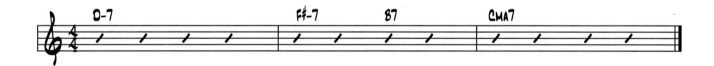

The Complete Guide To Improvisation

Ed Saindon

Constant Structure

This concept utilizes a specific type of chord that moves in equidistant intervals over the underlying harmony. The lines should repeat the same structure from chord to chord. Here are several examples illustrating this concept.

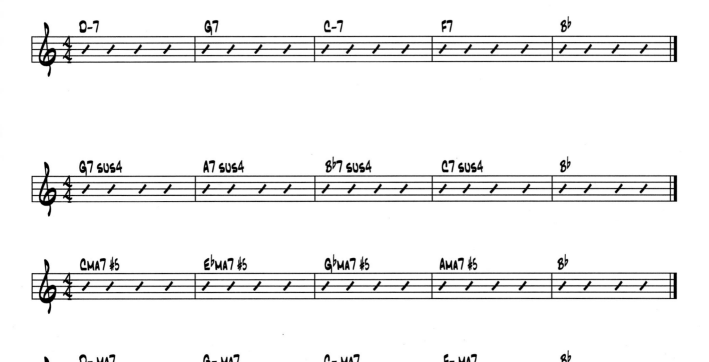

As evident by the examples illustrated in this section, there are many harmonic devices and concepts at the improvisor's disposal. These concepts should be explored with a variety of standard songs in order to be assimilated naturally in the improvisor's overall playing.

135

Chapter 5 • Harmonic Practices

Musical Examples

II-7 V7 Reharmonization Techniques

The following examples illustrate varying use of the Sub V7 and related II-7 resolving to the I chord. A line based on the Sub V7 over the G Dom 7 is utilized in Ex. 1E. However, the Sub V7 is treated as a Dom 7 sus and uses a Mixolydian b6 scale. (Ex. 1A - 1E)

Diminished Based Reharmonization of V7

Pay attention to the notes that are being sounded over the underlying harmony in the following examples. Also, notice that the chords are clearly spelled out in the line. Ex. 2D utilizes only the related II-7s and illustrates how the lines can sometimes sound stronger if the same inversions are used for the chord substitutions. (Ex. 2A - 2D)

Diminished Based Reharmonization of I Dim 7

Ex. 3A utilizes passing notes while still clearly sounding the F Dom 7 chord. Ex. 3B illustrates the use of motives and how not all of the chord tones of the substitute chords need be sounded. However, the substitute chords should still be clearly implied in order for the line to retain a sense of clarity and logic. Notice that example 3C uses approach and passing notes. (Ex. 3A – 3C)

Secondary Dominant – V7 of V7

This concept opens up many possibilities for reharmonization. Notice that Ex. 4C and Ex. 4D use only the related II-7s. Also notice the voice leading connection from chord to chord. In Ex. 4C the same inversions of the chords are utilized throughout, acting in essence as a motivic phrase and giving the line a sense of structure. (Ex. 4A - 4D)

Modal Interchange Chord Substitution

Modal Interchange substitutions can create a unique sound against the underlying harmony and the composition's tonality. The substitutions open up possibilities to create interesting lines over common II-7 V7 cadences. (Ex. 5A - 5E)

Harmonic Generalization

This concept is easy to apply. It allows the improvisor to simplify the changes, thereby making it an effective technique for fast tempo tunes, such as on up-tempo Rhythm Changes. (Ex. 6A - 6C)

Use of V7, Sub V7 and Related II-7s

This can be a valuable technique when playing on tunes with static harmony. The reharmonized chord changes can create interest via dissonance and added harmonic motion. As previously mentioned, the improvisor can utilize many improvisational techniques when sounding the reharmonized chord changes. Such possibilities include the use of Four Note Groupings, Pentatonic Scales, Symmetrical Diminished Shapes, etc. (Ex. 7A - 7D)

V7 b9 Alternation

This is an easy concept to apply and can be useful when one chord is maintained for an extended period, such as in modal tunes and vamps. Notice that Ex. 8C uses shapes from the Symmetrical Diminished scale based upon the A Dom 7 b9 chord. (Ex. 8A - 8C)

Approach Chords

This concept creates a strong moment of dissonance that is resolved with the sounding of the target chord. It is similar to Modal Interchange Chord substitution, except the list of approach chords is more expansive. (Ex. 9A - 9F)

Diatonic and Chromatic Passing Chords

This concept is conducive to creating dense lines, as in Coltrane's "sheets of sound". Both Ex. 10B and Ex. 10F use passing chords based upon the chromatic line cliché, from the root of the Dom 7 down to the b7th. (Ex. 10A - 10F)

Turnaround Variations

These are just a sample of the many turnaround variations that are possible. Some of the examples listed are more unorthodox and should be worked out ahead of time with the other band members if playing in a group. Other examples are more triadic in nature, which can sound more contemporary. Notice the use of different voicings on the Dim Maj 7 chords in Ex. 11G.

Note: Many other possibilities of turnarounds that utilize Sub V7s and related II-7s are not illustrated here. (Ex. 11A - 11H)

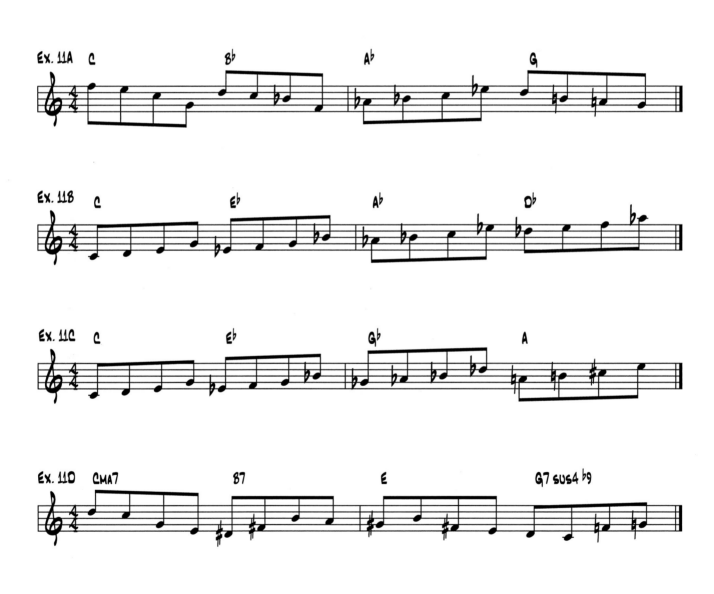

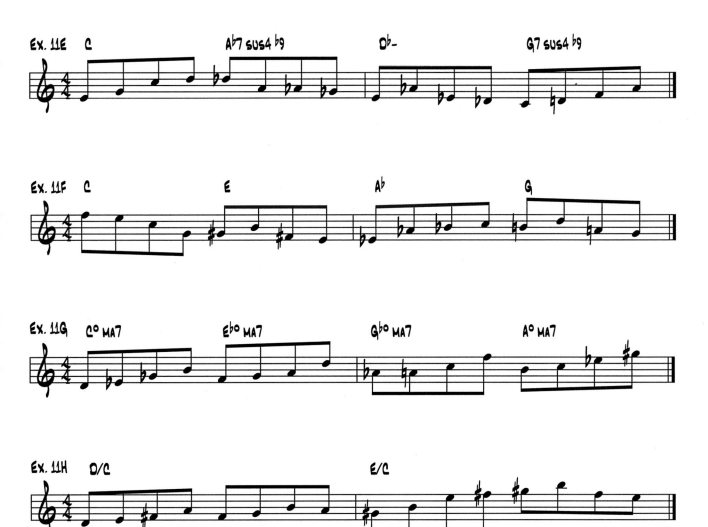

Use of Chromatic Lines

The use of chromatic lines can create harmonic motion over static progressions. The chromatic notes act as a thread in the overall line and should be clearly sounded. (Ex. 12A - 12C)

Chord Alteration

This is a harmonic practice prevalently used by many improvisors. It is an important concept that opens up many possibilities for creating interesting and unusual lines. When applying this concept, it is important to clearly sound the harmonic alteration and connect the lines via voice leading. It also helps if the lines utilize strong and identifiable melodic structures while sounding the chord alteration. In Ex. 13A the A Dom 7 is altered into an A Maj 7 #5 chord. The voicing of the Maj 7th #5 is a symmetrical structure (derived from the Symmetrical Augmented scale). It can also be analyzed as a Dim 7 approach (D Dim Maj 7, 9) to the D- chord. Ex. 13E is the application of chord alteration to the first 8 bars of a well-known standard. Notice how the chords are clearly connected. (Ex. 13A - 13E)

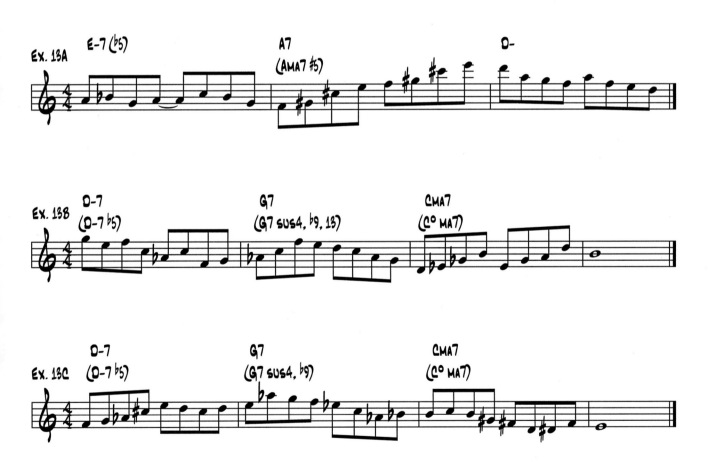

Harmonic Displacement

This is another common harmonic technique that can create momentary dissonance. The improvisor can experiment with using varying degrees of harmonic displacement. For example, anticipate a chord by a beat or two and then gradually increase the harmonic anticipation from there. (Ex. 14A - 14E)

Superimposition

There are a variety of harmonic techniques associated with superimposition that the improvisor can apply to standard chord progressions. Here are several options.

Extended Dominants

In order to effectively superimpose extended Dominants over various harmonic progressions, the improvisor should be able to sound lines that clearly outline extended Dominants. The following exercises should help in that regard.

Only one note need be changed in Ex. 15A in order to alter the character of the line. Different inversions of the chords could also be used. Ex. 15B illustrates the concept by using the b5th and the #5th in place of the natural 5th and the b9 in place of the root. A Bebop style line is achieved through the application of approach and passing notes in Ex. 15D. When utilizing approach and passing notes, try to make sure the harmonic intent is still clear. (Ex. 15A - 15D)

Note: Ex. 15A and Ex. 15B are exercises that should be played in all keys.

3 Tonic System

The application of the Three Tonic System can be an effective technique when properly executed, as it moves the lines out of the existing tonality of the chord progression. The lines should be clear and flow from one key to another. Notice the harmonic clarity in Ex. 16B even though a minimum of notes are used to establish the tonality of the three keys. (Ex.16A - 16B)

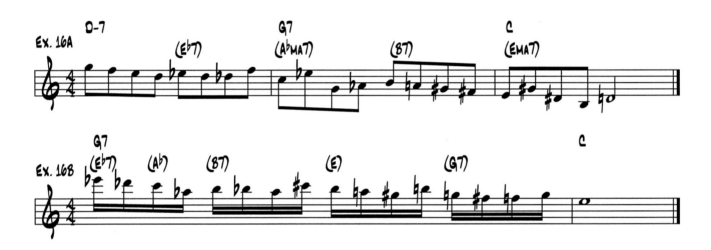

Parallel Tonal Substitution

This can be an effective technique, albeit a dissonant one. The concept can create a heightened level of dissonance while maintaining a sense of logic and direction in the line. (Ex. 17)

V7 or II-7 V7 Superimposition

In contrast with Bebop lines based over the original harmony, applying Bebop style ideas to superimposed V7s or II-7 V7s can help generate refreshing sounding lines. Keep in mind that the lines should clearly spell out the superimposed changes. This is also an effective technique for long periods of static harmony, as demonstrated in Ex. 18G. Throughout the examples, analyze which V7s and II-7 V7s were superimposed and pay attention to the various notes that are sounded by those specific superimpositions. (Ex. 18A - 18I)

Constant Structure

Constant structure chords function as strong identifiable motives that can move in and out of the underlying harmony. Notice the systematic transposition of the constant structure chords in the examples. For more information on a related topic, please refer to the Cyclic Patterns chapter. (Ex. 19A - 19C)

Knowledge of harmony is extremely important and beneficial for the jazz improvisor, since so many of the improvisational techniques and concepts are based upon harmonic principles. By simply applying the concepts in one's improvisation, even sporadically and on a limited basis, the harmonic techniques addressed in this chapter will go a long way.